A WORLD OF DIFFERENCE

- Northern Ireland
Edited by Angela Fairbrace & Vivien Linton

 Young**Writers**

First published in Great Britain in 2008 by:
Young Writers
Remus House
Coltsfoot Drive
Woodston
Peterborough
PE2 9JX
Telephone: 01733 890066
Website: www.youngwriters.co.uk

SB ISBN 978-1 84431 785 1

Foreword

Young Writers' Big Green Poetry Machine is a showcase for our nation's most brilliant young poets to share their thoughts, hopes and fears for the planet they call home.

Young Writers was established in 1991 to nurture creativity in our children and young adults, to give them an interest in poetry and an outlet to express themselves. Seeing their work in print will encourage them to keep writing as they grow, and become our poets of tomorrow.

Selecting the poems has been challenging and immensely rewarding. The effort and imagination invested by these young writers makes their poems a pleasure to enjoy reading time and time again.

Contents

Robyn Bell (14)   25
Laura Burns (13)   26
Aimee O'Higgins (14)   26
Sheena McCaugherty (14)   27
Aoife O'Rourke (14)   28
Emer Murtagh (14)   29
Ashling Thompson (14)   30
Lauren McCann (13)   31
Lauren Burns (14)   32
Fionnuala McConvey (14)   33
Orla Quinn (14)   34
Sarah Bryans (14)   34
Caron Maguire (14)   35
Niamh Winters (14)   35
Dearbhla Arkins (14)   36
Emma Rice (14)   37
Sorcha Rea (14)   38
Louise Monaghan (13)   39
Bronwyn Lam (14)   40
Louise Smyth (14)   41
Hannah Magorrian (14)   42
Eden Breen (14)   43
Angelica Kelly (14)   44
Shonagh Walsh (14)   45
Katie Bohill (14)   46
Emma Boyle (14)   46
Katherine Dowdall (14)   47
Lisa McMullan (14)   47
Rioghnach Bradley (14)   48
Sarah Grant (13)   49
Lauren McKernan (14)   50
Laura Mary Elizabeth Boden (13)   50
Erin Fitzsimons (14)   51

Beechlawn School, Hillsborough
Patrick McFerran (12)   51
Nicole Selfe (11)   52
Dean Watson (13)   52
Lewis Grant (13)   52

Carrickfergus Grammar School, Carrickfergus

Melissa Orr (12)	53
Matthew Brown (12)	53
Kelly Watson (12)	54
Josh Caldwell (12)	54
Matthew Davidson (12)	55
Emily Irvine (12)	55
Robert Boggs (12)	56
Adam Edgar (12)	56
Tayla Powell (12)	57
Jessica Allen (11)	57
Ross Hay (12)	58
Jason Armstrong (11)	58
Rebecca Mitchell (12)	58
Jordan Spry (11)	59
Sasha McAlister (12)	59
Ruth Nelson (12)	60
Peter Shepherd (12)	60
Aaron Elliott (12)	61

Christian Brothers School, Belfast

Patrick McGonigle (14)	61
Ryan Park (14)	62
Daire Gibbons (13)	62
Emmett Finnegan (13)	63
Mark Crilly (13)	63
Martin McLaughlin (14)	64
John Hay (14)	65
Patrick Ferry (14)	66

Dundonald High School, Dundonald

Leah Kelly (14)	66
Kurtis Davidson (14)	67
Lee Welsh (14)	67
John Nelson (14)	68
Lauren Wilson (14)	68
Bobbi Porte (14)	68
Aaron Graham (14)	69
Clarke Burns (14)	69

Glenlola Collegiate School, Bangor

Alice Hamilton (13)	69
Belinda Cree (14)	70
Emma McKee (14)	71
Jessica McKee (14)	72
Ciara Mallon (14)	72
Katie Glenn (14)	73
Lauran Brown (14)	73
Hannah McNamara (14)	74
Hannah Lindsay (14)	75
Brittany Smyth (14)	76
Laura Edwards (14)	76
Sarah Cheung (14)	77
Hannah Bulmer (14)	77
Amanda Huston (14)	78
Jennifer Storey (14)	78
Emma Coey (14)	79
Judith Aitcheson (14)	79
Rebecca McDowell (14)	80
Tammy Cosgrove (14)	81
Naomi Ellis (14)	82
Jessica Matear (14)	82
Sarah McVeagh (14)	83
Bronagh O'Loan (12)	83
Verity McDonald (15)	84
Lauren McGarvey (14)	85
Elizabeth Crawford (14)	86
Sarah McBride (14)	87
Holly Campbell (14)	88
Amy Mornin (14)	89
Lucia Devon (14)	90
Caroline Chambers (14)	91
Becky McCready (14)	92
Anna Thompson (14)	93
Lois Wheatland (14)	94
Olivia McIntyre (13)	95
Holly Milne (13)	96
Claire Smyth (13)	96
Charlotte McBride (13)	96
Nicole Kinder (13)	97

Limavady Grammar School, Limavady

Zoë Purvis (14)	97
Laura McLaughlin (13)	98
John McCready (14)	98
Karen Jones (14)	99
Niamh Fenlon (14)	99
Bosco McAuley (14)	100
Ryan Archibald (14)	100
Melissa Duffy (14)	101
Christopher McElreavey (13)	101
Maria Duddy (14)	102
John Fallows (14)	103

North Coast Integrated College, Coleraine

Amy Brussard (15)	104
Christine Cartwright (15)	106
Emily Brussard (15)	108

Omagh Academy, Omagh

Adam Burke (12)	109
Lindsay Hunter (12)	109
Sarah Moore (12)	110
Rachael Colhoun (12)	110
Bethany Kyle (12)	111
David Harpur & John Pak (12)	111
David Long (12)	112
Jamie Rankin (12)	112
Ryan Watt (12)	113

Rathfriland High School, Rathfriland

Lauren English (14)	114
Natasha Scragg (15)	115

St Benedict's College, Randalstown

Beverley Kirkpatrick (13)	116
Chelsea Stewart (13)	116
Samantha Ndebele (12)	117

St John's Business & Enterprise College, Dromore

Sinead Marlow (12)	117
Pauline McMenamin (14)	117
Ryan McElduff (12)	118
Roisin McGrade (14)	118

St Michael's College, Chanterhill

John Owens (12)	118
Eoin Dolan (12)	119
Mark Mulligan (12)	119
Christopher Flanagan (12)	120
Ruairí Doherty (14)	120
Eoín Baxter (12)	121
Ryan Carney (11)	121
Adam Breen (12)	122
Jason Donnelly (12)	122
James Britton (12)	123
Domhnall Boyle (12)	123
Patrick Dolan (14)	124
Jamie Antony Appleby (12)	124
Eddie Coutney (14)	124
Jack O'Dolan (12)	125
Tiernach O'Reilly (12)	125
Ciaran Monaghan (12)	125
Kevin Caulfield (14)	126
Liam Cassidy (14)	126
Ciaran Corrigan (12)	127
James Allen (12)	127
Oisin Corrigan (12)	128
Michael Cameron (12)	128
Jamie Farry (11)	129
Darragh Foy (12)	129
Niall Carson (14)	130
Kevin Fitzpatrick (12)	130
Barry Mulligan (12)	131
Cormac Valentine (12)	131
Oisin Clancy (14)	131
Rory Brennan (14)	132
Paul Donaghey (14)	132
Eoghan Corrigan (14)	133
Conor Doherty (14)	133

The Poems

Untitled

One piece of chewing gum soft and chewy
When finished put it in the bin.

Two packets of crisps wrinkly and noisy
When finished put them into a bin.

Three bottles of Coke round and tasty
When finished put them in the bin.

Don't drop your litter on the spot
Or you'll be fined a lot.

Don't throw your litter away
Keep our land cleaner day by day.

If we put it in the big green machine
Then we can keep our country green.

Stuart Moore (13)
Ashfield Boys' High School, Belfast

Untitled

Pollution is everywhere
Car fumes in the air,
Trash on the streets and in the seas.
We can save the planet by
Recycling and saving energy.
You can recycle by
Putting cans, paper and jars in the recycling bin.
You can save energy by
Putting turbines up for electricity.
You can put solar panels on your roof for heat.

Michael Cowen (13)
Ashfield Boys' High School, Belfast

Untitled

Why do you always take the car?
Why not walk down the street to the bar?
Pollution everywhere, destroying the planet
Recycling and saving energy can save the planet
So don't take a break,
It's a piece of cake!
More wind turbines for electricity
Solar panels on roofs for heat
No more fancy cars giving off car fumes.

Martin Allen (13)
Ashfield Boys' High School, Belfast

Go Green

We put bottles, cans and tins in the recycling bin
Don't throw your paper on the ground; put it in the recycling bin.
Reuse your plastic bags, reduce your waste,
Please do this to keep the planet green.
Instead of taking a car, walk to school,
Take a walk or a bike to places, use your car less.
Save your energy, turn your central heating down, turn it to 30^0.

Richard Hunter (13)
Ashfield Boys' High School, Belfast

Wouldn't It Be Great?

The world should be green
Like no other has seen
The air should be fresh
Not like a wretched breath
To reduce air pollution
We should think of new solutions
So let's get together and make our world safe
Put rubbish in the bin
Don't ruin what we are trying to create.

Jonny Kane (13)
Ashfield Boys' High School, Belfast

Our Planet

Grey and dark is our world
Pollution, smoking, car fumes, the lot
All we need is some recycling
And our planet can be green.
Some solutions to rid us of pollution
No smoking, more cycling, less driving cars
Or we might as well live on Mars.

Chris Crowe (13)
Ashfield Boys' High School, Belfast

Green Poem

Why not be green?
No need to be mean!
What did the Earth ever do to us?
Get out of the car and jump on the bus!

Don't drop litter in the street
You don't want it smelling all around *your* feet!

It says, 'Have a KitKat, have a break'
If you drop the wrapper, *you're* making a mistake!

Adam Auld (13)
Ashfield Boys' High School, Belfast

Being Green

Recycling bins are here and there
Polluting cars are everywhere!
We've got the solution
To get rid of pollution
Our streets will be cleaner
When we start being greener
Oh how lovely it will be!

Ian Patton (13)
Ashfield Boys' High School, Belfast

Saving Our Planet

Green, red and blue, recycling bins for you
Tins, paper and plastic
Can make something else fantastic!

If we drive our cars less
The ice won't melt and that's best
For penguins, seals and polar bears
To live, to play, to rest.

The Earth belongs to us all
So we should make our footprint small.
If we pedal instead of drive
It will help our world survive.

Ethan Hunsdale (12)
Ashfield Boys' High School, Belfast

A Green World

I dream of living in a green world
No more factories, no more cars,
No more smoking inside bars.

I dream of living in a green world
Eco-friendly lightbulbs, eco-friendly cars,
Eco-friendly inventions made by Man's great powers.

I dream of living in a green world
Will my dream come true
For a green world? It's up to me and you!

Clarke McGibney (13)
Ashfield Boys' High School, Belfast

Our Green Solution

In our world today we need to be greener
Leave the car behind, come out and be a runner.
Turn off unwanted lights
Make airports have less flights.
It's not too late to start
Get everyone to do their part.
We need to stop pollution
We've got to have a solution.
Let's get the world green
Let's keep it clean,
Stop sea levels rising
Stop the polar bears declining.

Ryan Hobday (13)
Ashfield Boys' High School, Belfast

Problems Of Today

Car fumes everywhere
No one seems to care
As much as we help the poor
There seems to be no cure
Stop littering and recycle more

Hearing the same stories becomes a bore
Global warming damaging us
Also the fumes which come off a bus
Is it too late to save us all?

Steven Storey (13)
Ashfield Boys' High School, Belfast

Shadow Of Sorrow

A broken old man lay in the shadows of a dark cobbled street
His life shown in deep wrinkles, adorning his pale sullen face
His stony blue eyes were empty
The eyes that had once shone glittering steel-blue
They were now soulless.

His face was as blank as a white sheet
His gaunt complexion and bones on show
They showed him as nothing more than an empty shell
The man who once was
There was nothing but sorrow behind that blank gaze.

Nothing but sorrow
Nothing inside him as he sat and thought
Thought of how he had been cast out of his once happy life
There was no happiness left
Not anymore.

He was now one of the forgotten
One of those people, the type people frowned on
The failures, the beggars, the outcasts.
He was now an outcast, detached from society
He wouldn't be a part of it again.

The life he had before had to be forgotten
He had to survive.
To get by and live with what he had.
Depending on the one person who looked at him on the street
Who looked, who gave a coin and took pity.

He sat in the corner
The cold wind chilling his frail form
The icy chill he felt each night
As he lay on the cold hard floor
As he tossed and turned in the cruel night air.

He prayed for the warmth of the sun
The sun to warm his bare skin
The skin that couldn't be covered by his rags
The stuff that others had cast out
Just like he had been.

But even a sunny day could not lift his spirits
Because the constant cloud of doom and misery will be there
Always, as he sat now in the shadow, the alleyway
He melted away into the shadow
He became part of the darkness.

Now one of them
The failures, the beggars, the outcasts
The lost and the forgotten
A shell of a man
Now faded to shadow.

Nicole Garrett (14)
Assumption Grammar School, Ballynahinch

Disease

Her eyes are swollen and she cannot see
She's about to drift off as her little girl clambers up upon her knee
'Mummy,' she says, 'are you still ill?'
'Yes, it's here forever,' she tells her, this in her own free will.
'Can the doctor not come and make your eyes better?'
'No, I don't have the money to send in a letter.'

Way later on during that night
She wakes up with a terrible shock,
She opens her eyes and she has lost her sight
As she sits there motionless, scared and sad
She wonders what her child will do as she hasn't even got a dad.
'How can this have happened?' she says with a sigh
Then her bottom lip trembles and she starts to cry.

That very next day around comes the doctor
He says that she got it from contaminated water.
Now her little child has to live in a home
And again the family that she loves has to leave her alone.

'My name is Sarah, I'm only thirty-three
And already my family have all had to leave me.'

Aishlinn McIlhone (13)
Assumption Grammar School, Ballynahinch

What Happens When Our Backs Are Turned

Children - too unfit to walk
Majority of them blind
Too unwell to talk
If you saw them, this you would find.

People sold as slaves
Made to work all day long.
They'll try to be brave
But this, I'm afraid, is no happy song.

Families torn apart
By the monster named Death.
Grief sinks to the bottom of their hearts
Cos of death, death, death.
This we know is unfair
Their lives have crashed and burned
The one thing I cannot bear
Is what happens when our backs are turned.

Aisling Lawson (14)
Assumption Grammar School, Ballynahinch

Poverty And War

Children hurting, children crying,
People killing, people dying,
What is this world turning into?
If you ask me, we don't have a clue!

Fragile and weak
They can hardly speak,
Pale and white
Hiding from the fight.

Food and water don't come easy
How can we sit back and be so lazy?
It's not fair, it's not right,
We have to stop this hard, hard life.

Laura McGeough (14)
Assumption Grammar School, Ballynahinch

Earth's Cry

I once looked down upon my surface
With a face that bore no shame,
Buildings taller than mountains
Lava hotter than flame.
Various different works of art
To benefit the human race,
Yet I now look down upon creation
With a different look on my face.
My sea was once as pure as snow
Varying from indigo to aquamarine,
My land dense with forest and flower
An eye-pleasing emerald-green.
But my view has now dimmed
My vision obscured
By a hazy grey cloud called pollution
But surely, I thought, *they will look after me*
The humans will find a solution.
I've provided them with a sky full of wonders
And a land full of fresh nutrition,
But instead of looking after their wonderful gift
Litter is the latest addition.
So it's litter that clutters my once-green lands
Litter that prevents it from breathing.
Litter that increases the humidity of my climate
A change which has left me seething.
Litter that has caused my seas to rise,
Polluting my ocean floor
Litter that brings a tear to my eye
Making it rain even more.
Litter that's finishing my animal kingdom
Extinction, one by one,
Litter that rips through my ozone layer
Increasing the intensity of the sun.
My eyes look upon the vastness of my planet
And they slowly fill with sorrow,
I wonder will things improve? Will the humans improve?
Will there be a better tomorrow?

Catriona Sloan (14)
Assumption Grammar School, Ballynahinch

Where Did It All Go Wrong?

Nothing matters anymore
The world just stands still
As I lie in my cardboard box
That shelters me from the evening chill.

I gaze up to the blackened sky
And listen to the silent sounds
Of the traffic in the busy streets
Dodging people that move around.

I wonder where it all went wrong
And what got me in this state.
Was it the drink, the drugs, the debt I'm in
Or is it simply down to fate?

I wonder, do my family care
Or even think of me?
While they sit in their cosy houses
Laughing, smiling and drinking tea.

My once new clothes, all tattered and torn
Begin to smell and stink
But where will I get the money from,
To buy that needed drink?

Life isn't easy when you're down and out
People walk by and ignore my shout.
Is it my clothes or my non-shaven face
That makes them consider me a total disgrace?

I'd love to turn back the years
And return to my beautiful wife,
But so much has happened in the past
I reckon I'll die living the homeless life.

Rebecca Mulholland (14)
Assumption Grammar School, Ballynahinch

A Game Of War

A little boy plays a game,
He plays a game of war.
Happy games in the playground,
Who could ask for more?

Leaders have a petty fight,
Play a game of war.
Shots in the head, thousands dead,
Who could ask for more?

Two teams run and hide,
Hands for their guns.
Bell rings, they give a moan,
Now their game is done.

Two teams, so much hate,
Tanks, bombs and guns.
End of day, they fight all night,
Their game is never done.

Teacher moans, bruised eye,
'We were playing a game,' he said.
Worried mother with a pack of ice
Sent him to bed.

Child moans, stray bullet,
'It was meant for a soldier,' he said.
Mourning mother, it ruined her life,
Now her son is dead.

Little boy plays a game
Plays a game of war.
Full-grown men with little sense
Who could ask for more?

Melanie McClements (14)
Assumption Grammar School, Ballynahinch

Poverty

The landscape is dry and harsh
The choking heat never stops
One goat is shared by one village
When will this painful lifestyle stop?

A well is shared but far away
Sometimes over five miles
The water is dirty and full of disease
There is always a risk of getting piles.

Pieces are scavenged
Scraps are boiled
The children are skeletal
Their bodies are spoiled.

The living conditions are cramped
Their house consists of one room
A kitchen, a bed and a table
Their life is nothing but gloom.

They have nothing to work with but a pencil
And school is two miles away
But they're different from us education-wise
They don't want to go home each day.

We have the facilities to help them
So why don't we put it to good use?
All they want is someone to say,
'We'll do our best to help you today.'

Rachel Bradley (14)
Assumption Grammar School, Ballynahinch

Like A Submarine In The Sea

The rain dashed down from the sky
That bounced hard off the ground
Everywhere soaked and everyone wet
It just kept falling down.

A sea of umbrellas was all you could see
Kids in welly boots jumping in puddles.
Cars couldn't drive, just sat useless
There was nothing anyone could do.

It just kept falling and falling
And it wouldn't dry away.
It kept getting higher and higher
No one knew what to do.

Cars began to swim away
House roofs were all you could see
Families in rubber boats,
Just waiting on help to come.

People swept out of their city
All because of lots of rain.
Police came and helped people out of trouble
Others had to swim to safety.

Months after the flood, people still not in their homes,
Having to live with friends and families.
Their town is underwater
Like a submarine in the sea.

Amy Townsley (14)
Assumption Grammar School, Ballynahinch

The Seasons

Each season takes its turn
With its own special weather that makes it fun.
But lately they've been changing
As the Earth is ageing.

They're getting mixed up
Because our ozone layer's not so tough.
Snow in spring
It's just not right, that's the thing.

But we are to blame
We broke the rules when playing the game,
We've been behaving badly for so long
That now it has all gone wrong.

In past summer days
When our ancestors used to play
They didn't know
That in summer days to come there would be snow!

But it's not too late
To change the Earth's fate,
If we all work together
We can change the messed up weather.

Chloe Kearney (14)
Assumption Grammar School, Ballynahinch

I'll Help Later . . .

As the scorching sun crosses the sky
The wealthy turn and won't hear their cry.
This marks the beginning of the eight-mile walk
Their mouths so dry they can barely talk.

I'll help later . . .

The water is dirty and dangerous too
They have to drink it but would you?
They drink out of bowls which alone they carved
Their leader doesn't care, he'll let them starve.

I'll help later . . .

The crops are ruined because it's just too hot
The water they carry is in a leaking pot.
Dangerous animals, a lack of food
No one will help them even though they could.

I'll help later . . .

Hunger, he reaches across the land
Mothers weep as death is at hand.
Their life is hard, they know no other way
Would you take their place even for one day?

Claire-Louise Magee (14)
Assumption Grammar School, Ballynahinch

Mundane Showers

Mundane raindrops fall upon delicate shoulders
The delicate shoulders of brutal war.
The shoulders that haughtily carry weapons of mass destruction
The shoulders that belong to the masters of battle
Battle, that drains through our lives open.

Mundane raindrops plummet upon these shoulders on the fighting line
The tip-tapping tremor on allied armour and soft skin
Bassoon, bazookas rocketing through the crisp smouldering air
Realising now that war is becoming as ordinary
As the very rainfall touching their fear-engulfed bodies.

Mundane raindrops tumble playfully among innocent children,
                                    naive in their freedom.
Playing folk tales of Prince Charming and beasts
While the real life beast of the battle
Prowls upon the babes' fiction and worlds.

Mundane raindrops collapse on lifeless souls
Drilling the beat of bullets into the twisted maze of our minds.
Murderers wishing to buy forgiveness
But paying the full price on their guilty consciences.

Mundane raindrops wash away the trudged-through mud
The puddles of blood and sweat.
The fear left in once-peaceful fields
Leaving behind guns and weapons and metal and blades
Showing the Earth's chronic, faltered form.

Mundane raindrops gracefully drop into our world
Smudging the visions of death and war from us
That clearly intend to stay in this life.
The killing virus of a shot, *bang!*
Dimming the star, the sun
Giving us hope that every day wars will disappear
Like those mundane showers of summer.

Evie Shaw (14)
Assumption Grammar School, Ballynahinch

Cancer

You don't see it coming
You have your whole life planned
One month you're fine
Then you have a death sentence

Your lips are getting paler
Your skin is hanging off
You're just skin and bones
And it tears me up inside to see you

Take a breath
I have to pull myself together
Don't understand why you have to go
Just counting down the days

Tears fill the eyes
And cries can be heard
I will not kiss you
Because the hardest part of this is saying goodbye.

Catriona McKeown (14)
Assumption Grammar School, Ballynahinch

The Animals Ask Why?

Why do you make us suffer?
Are we not like you?
Do we not have the right to live?
And give all that we can give?

Why do you cause us so much pain?
What have we ever done to you?
What gives you the right to lock us up and throw away the key
When we have the right to be free?

Why do you treat us so badly?
Why can't you just leave us alone?
Don't you have a heart?
If you did, you wouldn't tear us apart.

Eva Smith (14)
Assumption Grammar School, Ballynahinch

People Are Dying

Cold and wet they lie on the street,
No shelter, warmth or food to eat.

These people are invisible and we are stereotypical
To us they are just there and that's the way it is,
They are homeless.

The stick-thin bodies struggle to survive,
No money for medicine, needlessly they die.

Families grieve and mourn their loss,
Always knowing another life will be cost.

Dirty sewage water and a shack for a home,
How would you react, an understatement, a moan?

Flies walk all over their faces, their ribs stick out too far
These people need help, things should not be the way they are.

These people live in poverty.
Innocent creatures are slaughtered and shot
Their bodies are skinned and their fur is bought.
Tusks and horns are taken and sold
This isn't right, it does not deserve gold.

Fighting and killing, blood and death
Do we have to resort to this? It's not what's best.

During a war there is so much pain
If you think about it, there's nothing to gain.

What we need is world peace among all the races
So hold back your temper and show love on your faces.

People are dying; no one's doing their bit
So don't just sit there, get out and do something about it!

Niamh McGrath (14)
Assumption Grammar School, Ballynahinch

Killing In The Name Of Fashion

If you can put on that coat and still feel like a million dollars
Without thinking of the poor animal that suffered
Then I envy you

If you can stroke the soft fur that is keeping you warm
And not think of the poor animal it was keeping warm before you
Then I pity you

If you can look at the people campaigning for your help
And hear the stories of suffering and pain an animal goes through
And the cruelty they endure
And still reach for your purse to pay for that coat
Then I have no respect for you

But if you can put on that coat and see nothing but a dead animal
Who suffered for the sake of fashion
And if you can campaign to save that poor animal
Then I admire you and join you in your campaign to
Stop such ruthless killings.

Bronagh Murray (14)
Assumption Grammar School, Ballynahinch

Poverty

When I go into the bathroom I turn on the tap,
Somewhere, there are millions of people unable to do this way
across the map.
When I am tired, I hop into my bed
Somewhere, there are millions of people waiting to be fed.
When I flick on the TV I may see a performer and an audience giving
them a standing ovation
Somewhere, there are millions of people dying of starvation.
Often I wonder why we let this problem turn into a travesty
And I begin to doubt the morals of humanity.
I wonder why we let people live in poverty.

Emma Magee (14)
Assumption Grammar School, Ballynahinch

Homeless, Nowhere To Go

Nowhere to stay,
Nowhere to go,
When Daddy left us
We had no home.

Bus shelters, park benches
Is where we close our eyes to sleep.
Daddy gone, Mummy no job,
Therefore no money for our keep.

Passers-by stop and stare
With their clean clothes, designer shoes,
Their washed faces and cleanly washed hair.
They think they know how we feel,
They really don't have a clue.

Have they felt cold,
More than just a simple breeze?
Do they wear clothes like ours?
No! They only wear designer jeans.

Are their nights so cold that staying alive no longer matters?
Do they sit in a doorway thinking about life,
How their whole world is shattered?

They plan the next day and aren't even thankful they made it
through that one.

Naomi Magill (14)
Assumption Grammar School, Ballynahinch

Without A Home

Not having a home would be a nightmare
Imagine being a live laughing stock where strangers constantly
                                        stop and stare.
Nowadays society can be so vain and shallow,
They belittle those who have nothing, those whose cheeks are hollow
Slumped in the middle of a chaotic concrete jungle.
The worst noise we can hear is our child's tummy rumble.
Youthful pretty girls breeze by with their fancy shopping bags,
The only worry they have is dressing like the latest WAG.
Then there are the businessmen with their Armani briefcases,
They fire that spiteful look that hits like a bullet
They might as well spit in our faces.
I'm sure they couldn't imagine life without their luxurious luck
Drinking aromatic coffee and eating nutritious muffins from Starbucks.
My goodness, if they had to watch their beautiful child waste away
You would think they'd give you a few pounds to just about manage
                                        another day.
There's no point wanting to live the ideal life
Or wishing I could stay at home and brush my hair like they do on
                                        Desperate Housewives
Because that's not who I am, thank God, I know I have something.
I know where I have come from and where I have grown up,
I may not have a proper home but my flaws have made me
                                        more strong
The public flatter themselves thinking we want their sympathy
When I am thinking, *goodbye apathy, so long*.

Rebecca King (14)
Assumption Grammar School, Ballynahinch

Poverty

Life has stolen my golden shoes
But will not steal my smile
And will not take my dreams away
As I will be here for a while.

My crops outside may not be lush
Nor does my water flow free
But I have a life and a child
And poverty can't break me.

I can work, continue to strive
I'll keep on going and always provide.

The sky above doesn't breathe a word
Nor the cloud shed a tear
And no matter how I plead and pray
I'll never get out of here.

The sound of money I do not know
Nor the taste of fresh warm food
And even though they can help out here
I know they never would.

The sun above is beaming
Making my mouth so dry
And as I look at my beautiful baby
I wipe a tear from my eye.

Emma Power (14)
Assumption Grammar School, Ballynahinch

Poverty

Poverty is unbounded
And unbounded is fear
No means of help, comfort
Or relief in the near.

Disease and hunger linger in hand
The need for attention and care in demand.
No day will let pass without constant thought
Of the strain and neglect whilst left here to rot.

Never-ending despair of neglect and harm
Lost from the world and pushed from the people
For whose fault is it that they were not blessed
With the luxuries and life which we possess?

Aid will not tend and help is unwilling
No one seems to notice the unmerciful killing
Of those who are left to decay on the street.
The faceless, the unknown
The so-called 'dirt' at their feet.

Poverty is unbounded
And unbounded is fear.
Will the day come when everything is clear?
When people are noticed and all is restored?
When help is found and people are once more?
When all are equal and free from pain
Or is this just the reason why the people refrain?

Sarah Louise Carey (14)
Assumption Grammar School, Ballynahinch

Doing Our Bit

We treat the Earth like a rubbish dump
Putting litter where we want.
Plastic bags everywhere
But we don't care what we throw out.

We've become a race who depend on resources
For a comfortable lifestyle, no matter what the cost.
Frequent travel contributes to the greenhouse effect
Causing crops to fail and millions to starve.

Earth is precious and can't be replaced
So we need to act now for our children's sake.
Let's preserve our planet by doing our bit
What's done is done but it's never too late
So let's put it right *now!*

Mary Flanagan (14)
Assumption Grammar School, Ballynahinch

The Circus

The circus is a place to go to see silly clowns and daring acrobatics,
To watch roaring lions and galloping horses
But people forget the way those amazing creatures are treated
After the breathtaking shows.
When the curtain falls and everyone leaves for his or her home
The animals are locked in cages and left there until
                                        the next performance.
It's unfair as they are captured from their habitats
And from their open fields of freedom,
Every night they are made to perform under the sizzling spotlight
To amaze people from all around.
The animals long for the gentle breeze
And freedom to wander around aimlessly.
If only people knew the real pain these animals are in
And how they are missing their old and happy lifestyle.

Shauna McGreevy (14)
Assumption Grammar School, Ballynahinch

Poverty

Hunger and thirst, what would we know?
As we watch our plants grow and grow
Leaving our taps to flow and flow
Not thinking of all those whose supplies may be low.

I will not stand here and say
That it does not matter about all those that die every day
By drinking unclean water while we throw our food away
'Waste not want not,' isn't that what we should say?

People of all ages, young and old
Are dying every day in Africa that is what we're told
It is not hard to sponsor a child
So do it now while they are still alive.

I don't believe it to be fair
So get up and do something, don't act like you don't care
Help the people living in poverty to get their fair share
Tell everyone, everywhere!

Caroline O'Hare (14)
Assumption Grammar School, Ballynahinch

Water

Water is everywhere
But no one cares
Water is in our bath
But there won't be enough for the aftermath.
Water is used to make my dinner
But the dirty water is making the children thinner and thinner.
Water will go away someday
But what will all the people say.
Water can make some people die
But water can keep us all alive.

Robyn Bell (14)
Assumption Grammar School, Ballynahinch

End it now

Pollution is everywhere
As we can see,
Pollution is caused by cars, factories, waste materials
And even you and me!

Pollution by cars
Is one we all know,
Red light, orange light, green light
Go!

Smoke from exhaust
Drifting into the air
Causing acid rain
Without a care.

This is only one of the things
That pollutes the Earth all year round.
But with your help, it will be the only one
Without a doubt in my mind.

Laura Burns (13)
Assumption Grammar School, Ballynahinch

Litter

L itter's lying everywhere
I think we're all to blame
T oday, we don't even care
T ogether we should feel the shame
E ven though we all forget
R emember, we shall all regret.

Aimee O'Higgins (14)
Assumption Grammar School, Ballynahinch

Stitches

Night and day he slaves away
Without decent pay.
The same routine to his dismay
But then one bleak afternoon
He had a dream that wasn't to be any time soon.
In his mind he did ponder
Whether or not the customers wondered.

Who stands behind those shopkeepers' grins
Whose hands their money falls straight through and who wins?
Who is stuck with the vicious dagger of injustice time and time again?
Are those governments insane?
How many stitches hide greedy hands?
What's going on in those foreign lands?

He dreamed some more
For the thought had never occurred to him before
And in this dream he spoke loud and clear
For the whole world to hear.
To his delight he finally had a voice
This made those customers have a change in choice
He imagined worldwide workhouses no longer clustered
The WTOs were extremely flustered
His rights were no longer neglected
However his lifestyle was indeed affected.

Back to reality
And this harsh brutality
In his wages to his great fright
The package was oh so light
How would Mother pay the medical bills?
Baby Rosy might as well have been killed.

Sheena McCaugherty (14)
Assumption Grammar School, Ballynahinch

Brother

When that day comes
The day your brother wants to fight
To fight other brothers, fathers and friends
You will feel what I feel.

When you see that uniform
His freshly cut hair and blackened polished boots
With eyes full of innocence
You will feel what I feel.

When you think of the men
The men in charge who use others to fight their battles
Coveting other's lives
You will feel what I feel.

When those memories flood back
Of how your brother used to play with you
Giggling together, enjoying childhood
You will feel what I feel.

When you feel the warmth of that last hug
And your eyes fill with tormenting tears
Watching him board the plane
You will feel what I feel.

When you get that call
And you watch your mother crumple with the news
As you try to understand the pain deeply turning inside
Your heart aches and stomach churns
You will feel what I feel

When you look into those lifeless eyes
Your mother's sad lonely eyes
And you watch your mother deep in pain
As she has just lost part of herself
You will feel what I feel.

When you try to remember the happy times
When your brother and you played
And your mother had joyful eyes
You will feel what I feel.

But when your mind flashes back
And you once again feel the pain and anger
Unable to swallow as your eyes fill with tears
But until all this, all this pain
You will never feel what I feel.

Aoife O'Rourke (14)
Assumption Grammar School, Ballynahinch

The Burma Cyclone

No food, no water, no shelter to be seen,
My stomach is rumbling constantly.
My baby won't stop crying and my husband has gone
To get some food for our little son.

I can just see it now, my life flashing before my eyes,
My house has gone and my family have died.

I have heard of disasters such as this
But never believed it could happen to me.
It was so unexpected,
Why weren't we warned?
It would have made such a difference,
Now so many people have gone.

How selfish can they get?
We couldn't have stopped the cyclone
But could have avoided the effect.

One minute we're fine
The next we couldn't be worse.
Over twenty-two thousand lives just taken
As if they had no worth.

We're struggling on helpless
Like a bug on its back
Just searching for life
And even just the smallest bit of help.

Emer Murtagh (14)
Assumption Grammar School, Ballynahinch

The Chop

The rainforest has no voice
Nor anyone to speak for it.
Does anyone care
Not even a little bit?

A sight for sore eyes
The lush green leaves.
A place for monkey business
In the leaf-dressed trees.

The air we breathe
Is what they have made
And the crisp, cool leaves
Are great for some shade.

And how do we return the favour?
To the lush green leaves
Torn down from their branches
The leaf-dressed trees
Struck down with blades
And for what?

A dresser?
A door?
A table?
A floor?

The rainforest has no voice
Nor anyone to speak for it.
Does anyone care
Not even a little bit?

Ashling Thompson (14)
Assumption Grammar School, Ballynahinch

Homelessness

I sat in the dirty street
Cold, grey and dusty,
I gave a cough on the air
The wind, damp and musty.

They walked past me sitting there
Their eyes dark and glaring,
They scanned me there on the street,
They couldn't stop from staring.

The women held their children close
Old men shook their heads.
I'd love to live their simple lives
But I live mine instead.

My clothes are torn and tattered,
My body cut and smelly,
I search for any decent food
I can put into my belly.

A life like this is to be lonely
No job, no family, no fun.
I know I've not the best life
But I know it's not the worst one.

I'm thankful for the clothes on my back
The little things that are mine,
I'd never be one of them
Who pass me all the time.

They care not for what they have
Care not for those in bad ways.
Homelessness is nothing; I have love in my heart
And I'd take that any day.

Lauren McCann (13)
Assumption Grammar School, Ballynahinch

Going, Going Gone!

The rainforest, a big and wonderful sight
Full of amazement, empty of fright.

The birds and the trees, so happy and bright
So full of colour even in the black of night.

The gushing waterfalls, flowing as one
Will never stop flowing until the job is done.

The small scared animals, cowering alone
Their environment has been destroyed as has their home.

The hidden forest tribe, hide behind their spears
As their wild suspicions confirm their fears.

The builders in hard hats just doing their job
Destroying the rainforest, no doubt or fear at all.

We all seem to think something should be done
But no one acts, not a soul, no one.

But for the rainforest and its friends, time is running out
We listen to the people roar and shout.

If we don't act now though we've waited so long
The rainforest will be going, going, gone!

Lauren Burns (14)
Assumption Grammar School, Ballynahinch

One Lucky Shot

I live today but could die tomorrow,
That's what it's like for a life full of sorrow.

With my mother in front and my brother behind
I run through the land with visions of death stuck in my mind.

These hunters, how cruel their life must be,
To take revenge on an animal like me.

I hear one shot and then another,
I turn and look at my dead brother
Then turn around to my sad mother.

She signals to me to go on
And in a moment she too is gone!
Of my family, two I have lost,
What a price, what a cost?

Fur like mine would pay a lot
And all it takes is one lucky shot.

How can I go on with my family gone
How can you not see the pain you inflict on me?
But I must go on with a life full of sorrow
Living in fear of you coming back tomorrow.

Fionnuala McConvey (14)
Assumption Grammar School, Ballynahinch

Street Life

The sun would set, the sun would dawn
My eyes would blink and I'd let out a yawn.
Days and days would pass me by,
All I could do was lie and lie.
Hundreds of people would walk right past
If only they knew how long it would last.
A small twenty pence would mean so much
But now that I'm dirty, strangers lose touch.
Night-times are worse, so I lie in fear
Awaiting the thug who may soon appear.
But once they are over a new day starts
And there is a chance I could meet a loving heart.
Miracles can happen and hopefully to me
So I wish for this and the day I'll be free.
Now all I can do is hope for the best
Maybe someone else will sort out the rest.

Orla Quinn (14)
Assumption Grammar School, Ballynahinch

The Poor Dog

How could you do that?
Instead of giving your dog a pat
You give it a whack!

The dog sits in the corner
Hoping that you don't come back
To give it another whack.

And once you get sick of it
You go and tie it to a bin,
Now that is just a sin.

How could you do that?
Instead of giving your dog a pat
You give it a whack!

Sarah Bryans (14)
Assumption Grammar School, Ballynahinch

War Is Everywhere

Houses burnt beyond repair
Women weeping in despair
Bombs fly across the sky
Another family's turn to die.

Children looking to the sky
Tears drying on their face
Families lie in shallow graves
A nation sore of bitter disgrace.

Children afraid to even cry
Silently suffering wonder why.
Deathly gases fill their lungs
There is nowhere to hide, nowhere to run.

Their aid is always late
Women and girls kidnapped and raped.
Some choose to accept fate
Generations filled with hate.

Caron Maguire (14)
Assumption Grammar School, Ballynahinch

Pollution

Smelling gases in the air,
Choking, coughing everywhere.

Car fumes pollute the street,
The rubbish from what we eat.

Walk along the dirty path,
See the mess but do not laugh.

Clean streets should be our pride
With empty bins side by side.

The dirty streets, the dirty air,
We should *all* really care!

Niamh Winters (14)
Assumption Grammar School, Ballynahinch

Animal Cruelty

God made all the animals
That on this Earth do dwell
And just like human beings
They should be treated well.

St Francis of Assisi
Was a saint from Italy
He cherished every animal
Every bird and every bee.

We should all obey his lesson
And treat animals with care
From the smallest little insects
To the biggest grizzly bear.

Animal cruelty exists
Throughout the world today
But in our civilised society
No part it should ever play.

All animals should be cared for
Domestic and wild alike
We should never lift our hand or foot
An animal to strike.

Dearbhla Arkins (14)
Assumption Grammar School, Ballynahinch

Poverty Or Wealth?

The money, the fashion, the sparkles, the gold,
Expensive coats to shield the cold.
Sunday feasts and champagne nights,
Money to throw on gambling fights.

The torn clothes, the burning sun,
To fetch water, there're miles to run.
Tired and hungry, worried and sore,
We know not of comfort, we sleep on the floor.

The job in the city, the company car,
Holidays abroad, travelling far.
Designer labels, the latest hairstyles,
Money stacked up, piles upon piles.

Do you know the feeling of starvation?
No money for school means no education.
People dying everywhere,
Hunger, disease, do you think it's fair?

Many eyes are shut to this poverty
Not seeing the harsh reality.
But if you look, you will find
It's surprising how you could be so blind.

Emma Rice (14)
Assumption Grammar School, Ballynahinch

The Homeless

They sit on the street
On a cold winter's night,
As people rush by
We know it's not right.

The hunger in their eyes
Their ice-cold stare,
We can go home
But they'll always be there.

They may cross your mind
You might think of their strife,
But soon you'll walk by
And get on with your life.

Should we ignore them
Their pain and their cry?
As they think of the people
Who walk right on by.

Why do they lie there?
Who is to blame?
They are ordinary people,
We are all just the same.

Sorcha Rea (14)
Assumption Grammar School, Ballynahinch

Street Corners Of Belfast

People lying spread out along Belfast's streets
No food, no water, just a rug to cover their knees.
As the wind howls and the rain beats down
They clamber into an alleyway for shelter.

The public stop and stare sometimes
But are too afraid to give them money.
Why are these people to be left starving and thirsty?
There's no help, no help from anyone!

A man sits lonely on a street corner
With a rough beard and not a wash in weeks.
He has a coat, a rug and one shoe
Oh what a life this man lives.

A woman sits lonely on a street corner
A young baby held in her arms
She holds out her hand for money
But the people just walk on by.

As we sit in the warmth of our houses
These people are left out in the cold
The young and the old are both suffering
We must take everything for granted as they lie along Belfast's streets.

Louise Monaghan (13)
Assumption Grammar School, Ballynahinch

Twenty Questions

Can you see their pain?
Can you hear their cries?
Do you know how they feel
When their own bullet flies?

We're fighting a war
That no one can win,
As we shoot at each other
And do ourselves in.

The end of the world
Is coming they say.
But humanity's gone
At the end of the day.

Who's waging this war?
Who's telling the lies?
Who's giving the guns
To the youngest of guys?

What good does this do?
Does it help us at all?
How can we stand just to watch
Others fall?

How do we run
From the things we've done?
How does one sleep in the night?

Why can't I cry?
Am I frozen inside?
Could we fix it
If we lived, if we loved, if we tried?

A mother, a father, a brother, a son
All it takes is a shot
And their world is undone.

The world is shattered,
It's torn apart.
My own life is ending,
It's breaking my heart.

If the war was all over,
If the people were dead,
Could I face what's going
On in my head?

So I'll ask you a question
Say, let's fight a war,
What is the cause we're fighting for?
Do you help or you harm?
Do you care?

Can you see their pain?
Can you hear their cries?
With every shot that we fire
Each one of us dies.

Bronwyn Lam (14)
Assumption Grammar School, Ballynahinch

Pavements

What do you feel when you see them in the street?
The ragged beggars with the stale, musty smell
All they need is shelter to be loved
To have something the fortunate take for granted.

Many have suffered from debt, lost a car, even a family
They unfortunately are born into this
They must struggle for survival
Empty nights, falling asleep on dirty pavements.

Are you hungry? No, you're not.
The hunger you feel may be satisfied in minutes
They may wait hours for a crumb
A crumb to keep their weak bodies form fading.

Are you happy? They're not.
Would you trade situations, I think not.
Look at your life, look at theirs, compare. Think. Love. Help!

Louise Smyth (14)
Assumption Grammar School, Ballynahinch

Homeless

Day and night
All year round
People sleep
On the black pavement ground.

No money to spend
No food to eat
Starving is the way
These people live each day.

They wake up each morning
And go to sleep each night
With dreaded thoughts about the following hours
And no bed to lie their poor little heads.

As summer comes, winter ends
These people's lives do not change
Unhappy and neglected is how they feel
Out in the season's cold air.

Their friends have been lost
And unable to fend
So they continue living unwanted
On the cold, black pavement around.

There is nothing we can do
Apart from say a little prayer
And hope that one day
God will answer with gentle, loving care.

Hannah Magorrian (14)
Assumption Grammar School, Ballynahinch

I Guess It's Your Own Decision

Do you feel comfortable in this world within?
It seems that respect is impossible to win.
People are suddenly just judged because of their colour of skin.
Racism leads to division
I guess it's your own decision.
As humans ignore it, it drives me to despair
As racism is around us everywhere.
We live in a so-called democracy
But to be honest, racism will never be set free.
Racism leads to division
I guess it's your own decision.
It's not fair
People just don't seem to care
Should we continue to live in a world where they discriminate?
Just because they're from different countries
Is there really a need to dictate?
Racism leads to division
I guess it's your own decision.
For equality in this world does not seem to take place
Judged continuously because of their race.
Fight for what is right
Racism leads to division
I guess it's your own decision
Some people are not aware
Of the racism around us everywhere.
It leads to division
I guess it's your own decision.

Eden Breen (14)
Assumption Grammar School, Ballynahinch

Stop!

The dark, black hole
never-ending.
The words, shouts, remarks -
never-ending.
The feeling of hopelessness
will haunt you forever.

How would you feel
If you were snarled at,
abused, spat at, scorned
and you were only a
different kind of human being?

How would a child feel?
A young person?
An adult?
Would it be different?
Will it ever go away?

We should believe that everyone is equal,
everyone in the world is the same.
Treat everyone as you would like to be treated
- isn't that what's written?

There are thugs out there
the unfriendly friends
mean monsters
nasty natives
offensive others.

Have you ever wondered?
Maybe we might be the other,
we are all guilty
of racist comments.
Racism is bad!
Learn to say *stop!*

Angelica Kelly (14)
Assumption Grammar School, Ballynahinch

Pain

Seasons are changing
Waves are crashing
Stars are falling just like us
Days grow longer and nights grow shorter
Can't you see their pain?

Look out across the water
Faces of lonely daughters
And mothers who care
They just can't be there.

Picking up the pieces
Of a life that's broken
Stitching it together
With the seams wide open.

You keep crying
Till you cannot see at all
You keep crying
Till you cannot breathe at all
And now that I'm strong
I have figured out
This world turns cold
And takes effect on my soul.

Well, it's never going to get me
I'm like a bullet through a flock of doves
Well, it's never going to catch me
I'm like air going through our gloves.

Shattered glass and flames
Snapshots of reality
Burnt pictures and memories
Their hearts turn to grey.

What do you do when they give you a smack?
What do you do when they don't come back?
What do you do when no one's home?
What do you do when you're all alone?
Out of control, now on your own
Pain!

Shonagh Walsh (14)
Assumption Grammar School, Ballynahinch

Water Is Everywhere

Water is everywhere
But do we really care?

We need it to quench our thirst
We need it to come first
We need it for our necessities
We need it for our recipes

People in Africa have water
But does it feed their sons and daughters?

For years they have tried and tried
But they still walk miles and miles
They miss out on an education but will it benefit their nation?

Instead of receiving pure water
They receive dirty water
Will this keep them alive?
Will this make them strive?

Water is everywhere
But do we really care?

Katie Bohill (14)
Assumption Grammar School, Ballynahinch

Injustice

Tears, roars, screams,
Sounds of dying soldiers in battle.
Tears, roars, screams,
Sounds of grieving mothers.
Cheers, roars, screams,
Sounds of military leaders celebrating.
Cheers, roars, screams,
Sounds of our president laughing.
There are no winners or losers
No right or wrong
Only young innocent lives being lost.

Emma Boyle (14)
Assumption Grammar School, Ballynahinch

Learning To Change

War can come and war can go
But the damage that's left is there to show.
The heartache, the suffering,
The homeless, the poor,
Why can't we just learn to share?

Learn to forgive,
Learn to forget,
Learn to live,
And not to regret.

For our world needs to change
It needs to be right,
Not to kill
And not to fight.

So no more fighting
And no more killing,
Just a peaceful world
Where everyone is winning.

Katherine Dowdall (14)
Assumption Grammar School, Ballynahinch

Poverty

People in their big houses
People in their fancy cars
Why can't we all be the same?
Who is to blame?

So many people in the world today
Are suffering from poverty
What can they do?
Please donate a few.

You can make a huge difference
If you phone a charity today
All you have to do is make a right choice
And many in the world today will rejoice!

Lisa McMullan (14)
Assumption Grammar School, Ballynahinch

Street Corner Blues

Do you ever take notice
As you're walking on past
Of the man in the corner
Who is wasting away much too fast?

With a cup in one hand
He silently pleads
In hope that someone
Will help tend to his needs.

Do you ever wonder
What life would be like
If that space in the corner
Was where *you* spent the night?
If your possessions were limited
To other's unwanted goods
And your diet consisted
Of rancid rotten food?

Have you ever considered
This homeless man's feelings?
Although his possessions
Are small and few
He has feelings
Just like you.
Dreams, hopes and wishes
He has many
But no home, no comfort
Not even a penny.

Rioghnach Bradley (14)
Assumption Grammar School, Ballynahinch

Homeless

It started so simple
Like a tumour disguised as a pimple
An acorn beneath the soil
One hidden mustard seed among the bulbs.

A tiny disagreement
She lost her religion
Throwing her screams and heart
At me in the kitchen.

They'd had enough
For I was just
A parasite nibbling away
At the back of their brain.

So now I'm alone
Hugging myself in the mall doorway
As shoppers walk by
The same every day.

I used to be like them
Struggling in the Christmas rush
But now I'm not
I'm worthless, poor, dirty, a tramp!

For nobody loves me
And nobody has
Since that day
I became homeless.

Sarah Grant (13)
Assumption Grammar School, Ballynahinch

Recycling

Landfill sites getting bigger
The ozone layer getting weaker
Glass and papers everywhere
Tin cans and bottles on the floor
We need to recycle
We need to clean up.

Plastic bags in the ocean
Deserted clothes and shoes
Perfect to make something new
Empty recycling bins
In need of rubbish
Cans and bottles and the morning paper!

A can made into something new
A paper to a pen
Tin cans and bottles used again
We are recycling
Landfill sites getting smaller
The ozone layer getting stronger.

Lauren McKernan (14)
Assumption Grammar School, Ballynahinch

Hell On Earth

A bomb explodes
But no one blinks an eye
Can you not hear this country cry?

Soldiers go on
With weapons in their hands
Marching through the devastated lands.

Why is this happening
Will someone not tell?
Why has Earth suddenly become Hell?

Laura Mary Elizabeth Boden (13)
Assumption Grammar School, Ballynahinch

Choke

That's what you're doing to us
With your car exhausts.
Poisoning the environment
With those horrible chemicals
Ruining the lives
Of generations to come.

Melting!
Those Polar ice caps
Raising sea levels
Surely some countries will drown!
Polar bears and penguins
Where will they go?
All because we are too busy
Caught up in our own lives
Globalised murder!

Erin Fitzsimons (14)
Assumption Grammar School, Ballynahinch

Pollution

Dirty people, dirty towns,
Some clean people, some clean towns.
Rubbish here, rubbish there
Sometimes I see rubbish everywhere.
I hear bin lorries all over town
I smell the dump on a sunny warm day
I taste a bittersweet aroma of rotten food and decaying animals
I touch the rubbish when I put mine in the bin.

Patrick McFerran (12)
Beechlawn School, Hillsborough

Clean Our Streets

R ecycling is good.
E veryone knows that they should
C lean up the streets by putting rubbish away.
Y ou can do it today!
C ollect all the tins.
L eave the park with clean bins.
E veryone do their bit, please!

Nicole Selfe (11)
Beechlawn School, Hillsborough

Litter

Litter is bad and litter is sad
Litter sometimes gets in your hair and sometimes your chair
Litter is not cool because litter is cruel
A punk litters and a punk is a hunk of junk
Litter is no fun, litter blocks the sun
Litter is for a bin, litter does not make you win.

Dean Watson (13)
Beechlawn School, Hillsborough

Rainforest

The rainforest looks like a colourful peacock
The rainforest feels like a jungle
The rainforest sounds like a zoo
The rainforest smells like freshly cut grass
The rainforest tastes like pineapples.

Lewis Grant (13)
Beechlawn School, Hillsborough

Your Street

Walking down the footpath
An awful sight I see
Scribbles and drawings
In markers and pens
Covering the walls in graffiti.

Walking down the footpath
The streets are dark as night
As stones get thrown
And glass gets broken
Leaving the streets with no light.

Walking down the footpath
A lovely sight I see
Clean painted walls
And bright streets at night
I know where I'd rather be!

Melissa Orr (12)
Carrickfergus Grammar School, Carrickfergus

Recycling

R educe, reuse and recycle
E asy as ABC
C ans, bottles and paper
Y es, we can recycle it all
C ollecting could not be easier
L andfills are going to starve
I nto the bins the rubbish goes
N ow is the time to get started
G reen is the way to go.

Matthew Brown (12)
Carrickfergus Grammar School, Carrickfergus

Hunting

I feel sorry for all those animals who were shot
For their horn, skin or the lot.
No wonder there's so many species dying out
Do hunters do it for the fame or the shout?
To have to go through that pain
It must be absolutely insane.
Those poor animals doing no harm
For the hunters there's a charm.
I don't know how hunters live with the guilt
Something I would never like to feel or have felt.
To take a life just like yours or mine
Definitely no reason to shine.
What's so special about skin or a horn?
To take them, it's just another life torn.
I think hunting should be banned
This is where I will always stand.

Kelly Watson (12)
Carrickfergus Grammar School, Carrickfergus

Recycling Heroes

Monday morning, what's that sound?
It's the Bryson heroes coming round.
They're here to rescue kerbie bin
Reuse, recycle, whatever's within.
Their brysonmobile hits the street
Just like policemen on their beat.
Looking for villains committing the sin
Of using the big black wheelie bin!

Josh Caldwell (12)
Carrickfergus Grammar School, Carrickfergus

Alone Without A Home

If you were alone and had no home
You really would be sad,
If you were not alone and had a home
You really should be glad.
You couldn't imagine the pain
When you wake up again and find you're not in bed,
It could be caused by poverty, war or even natural disaster
When people have no homes it's usually Mother Nature who has
proven she is master.
You can help these people by donating today
People could rebuild their houses and forget yesterday
These people will be happy and you will be too
Whether you donate or not, the choice is up to you.

Matthew Davidson (12)
Carrickfergus Grammar School, Carrickfergus

Racism

I wish I could go back in time, way, way back
To what's yours was mine,
Where the world was black and white
And people got on without a fight.
But now everything's changed
What's mine you steal!
The world can't handle being black and white
No one gets on, there's always a fight.
This isn't how it should be
This isn't right,
Can't we just accept
That you're black and I'm white?

Emily Irvine (12)
Carrickfergus Grammar School, Carrickfergus

My Pride And Joy

My pride and joy sitting in the garden
So pretty sitting there
I can't wait to show my friends
They'll be so jealous
I just can't wait.
Oh no, it's nearly midnight
I must go to sleep now
Goodnight my pride and joy.

Time to get up
Good morning pride and joy
Oh no!
What has happened?
My pride and joy wrecked!
Broken!
Smashed!
Ruined!

Vandals, I tell you, vandals have done this.
They have no respect for anything,
They think everything is there to be ruined
And that everything belongs to them.

Robert Boggs (12)
Carrickfergus Grammar School, Carrickfergus

Being Homeless

Being homeless isn't nice
You sleep beside the rats and mice.
Your home is in a cardboard box
And you can't afford a pair of socks.
There's no PlayStation nor TV
No DS Lite nor MP3.
You need to beg by day and night
For money so you can get a bite.

Adam Edgar (12)
Carrickfergus Grammar School, Carrickfergus

Man

Our beautiful world is in jeopardy and who is to blame . . . Man!

Greedy Man
He burns the rainforests and destroys animals and rare plants
                                                to gain more and more land.
Reckless Man
He allows chemical to pour into rivers killing thousands of fish
                                                                and wildlife.
Evil Man
He emits smoke and toxic fumes into the atmosphere
                                                causing pollution.
Ego Man
He is and has been responsible for all wars.

Neanderthal Man
He hunts animals into extinction, not for food but furs, teeth, tusks
                                                and bones for magical potions.

Wake up Man before our world comes to an end!

Tayla Powell (12)
Carrickfergus Grammar School, Carrickfergus

The Forest

The forests are losing their trees
And the little bees.
The animals are losing their homes
While you're on the phone
That's why I'm here to say
Do not stay away.
Come with me
And you will see
This little world of ours
Is about to fall at a mighty power!

Jessica Allen (11)
Carrickfergus Grammar School, Carrickfergus

Waste Disposal

Glass, plastic, metal tin cans
All of this can make up the land.
If into the bin lorry it goes
It could end up under our toes.
The recycling box is the only direction
For this assortment of collection.
All of this and much more
Can keep the bin lorry away from your door.

Ross Hay (12)
Carrickfergus Grammar School, Carrickfergus

Litter

The streets are aglow with litter
Which makes the people quite bitter
Put it in the bin
It might help your kin
And help make our planet much fitter.

Jason Armstrong (11)
Carrickfergus Grammar School, Carrickfergus

Racism

Racism is bad
It makes me mad
To see people sin
Just because of the colour of someone else's skin.
So why can't we all just love one another?
'Cause after all, black and white is just a colour.

Rebecca Mitchell (12)
Carrickfergus Grammar School, Carrickfergus

Guess What I Am?

Guess what I am?
I am . . .
Selfish
Worthless
A waste of space
Stupid
Strange
An understatement
A brat
Good for nothing
Unloved
Guessed yet?
I'm abused!
These are the words my abuser uses towards me,
The words I'm beginning to believe.

Jordan Spry (11)
Carrickfergus Grammar School, Carrickfergus

Cool Or Fool?

You think you're cool
But you're really a fool.
Dropping litter by the road
Giving wardens quite a load.
Eating sweets and crisps and treats
Then the wrappers lie at your feet.

You think you're cool
But you're really a fool.
So don't drop litter anymore
And it will open a new door
To making our world a better place
And changing the look on our warden's face.

Sasha McAlister (12)
Carrickfergus Grammar School, Carrickfergus

Rhino Extinction

Why, oh why, oh why
Do rhinos have to die?
They're going to be extinct
If people don't start to think!

The poachers come out at night
And give the rhinos a fright
But nought is there to see
As the poachers that came before
Killed the very last of them.

So only a few remain alive
But will they for much longer?
So why, oh why, oh why
Do rhinos have to die?

Ruth Nelson (12)
Carrickfergus Grammar School, Carrickfergus

Global Warming

No more ice caps
No more glaciers
No more polar bears
Who cares?
I do!
Some recycling
Some less CO_2 emissions
Some more hybrid engines
A lot more changes
I can do it
So can you!

Peter Shepherd (12)
Carrickfergus Grammar School, Carrickfergus

Poverty

Poverty is bad
It makes people sad
When you have no money
And can't even afford honey
It makes people sad
Poverty is bad.

Poverty is bad
It makes me glad
That I have money
To spend when it's sunny
This makes me glad
But poverty is bad.

Poverty is bad
You should be glad
Because you've got lots of goods
And plenty of food
You should be glad
But poverty is bad.

Aaron Elliott (12)
Carrickfergus Grammar School, Carrickfergus

Homeless

Why did it happen to me,
How could I have been so stupid?
If only I had one more chance
I could get my life on track.
I wouldn't be lying here shivering
Where no one cares, I'm just dead to them
My family hate me and it's all my fault.
It's your choice to control you life
Do *you* want to be homeless?

Patrick McGonigle (14)
Christian Brothers School, Belfast

War

Before the war it was peaceful and fun
You could play football in the park in the hot sun.
You could walk on streets at any time
And jump and play and sign and rhyme.

The buildings stood up straight and strong
The streets were clean all day long.
We walked and jumped the kerbs in peace
Before our country went to war.

Our country is not at peace anymore
We can't play in the park anymore because of the terrible war.
We can't walk the streets singing
Without the fear of a bullet's ting.

The buildings are flattened to the ground
Because of the bombs and the pound, pound, pound!
There are bullets all over the place
And not a single happy face.

Ryan Park (14)
Christian Brothers School, Belfast

The Homeless Teenagers!

Being homeless is really a nightmare
Having nowhere to go, no home, no lair.
Having nothing, begging for money
Walking about looking for some honey.
Lying there, nothing to do
But you're still dreaming of eating stew.
Hopefully you'll find somewhere to stay
Before you must put your head on a bale of hay.
Thrown out of the house for being bold
And now I'm damp and seriously cold.

Daire Gibbons (13)
Christian Brothers School, Belfast

The War

The green grass on the plain
The bright flowers blowing in the wind
The silent sound of peace
The heroes are no longer
Standing head held high.

They would be have been amazed at the sight I see before me
Calm and still, not like before
Bombs no longer dropping
No guns firing now
They would have been proud
To see what they achieved.

The sky was getting darker
I decided I should go
They didn't come with me
They stayed standing still
Like flowers on a window.

Emmett Finnegan (13)
Christian Brothers School, Belfast

Why Drop It?

L itter, litter, why drop litter?
I t's all a bunch of rubbish!
T ime to stop throwing your juice away
T ell them all to stop today!
E at it up and stick it in your pocket
R un to the nearest bin as fast as a rocket!

Mark Crilly (13)
Christian Brothers School, Belfast

Racism

Black or white, it shouldn't really matter
We all have the right to food and water.
People are dying but more people are crying
We all have the same needs,
We should be treated the same
Without blame.
People are afraid to go out
Others will shout
Others live with pride
And take it all in their stride.
For peace to happen we need to unite
And not punch or fight.

People run about with racist thoughts
But these are easily bought
Some say it's alright to discriminate
Others say it's OK to differentiate.
In my view everyone is equal but it's your view that counts.

Martin McLaughlin (14)
Christian Brothers School, Belfast

Ruined Dreams

Racism is the worst thing
People look at me as if I'm nothing
I eat, I sleep, I do it all
I try and impress them
But my hopes just fall.

They ruin my dreams; I could just scream and scream and scream!
It's a crime but I'm doing the time.

Why does it matter if I'm black, white or Chinese?
We are all the same, no one is to blame.

I wish for a world without hurt,
A place where I don't feel like dirt
We are all equal and should treat each other as people.

They say it's a dog-eat-dog world with everyone for himself
Why can't you see you are leaving me to dwell in fear
When all I can do is shed a tear?

I know who I am I know I am strong
But all these people think because I'm white that everyone
treats me alright.

John Hay (14)
Christian Brothers School, Belfast

Racism

Why does everyone call me black?
Others say we all smoke crack!
Other people say the same things too,
They are just like me and you!

Why does everyone call me brown?
Others say we always frown!
Other people say the same things too,
They are just like me and you!

Why does everyone call me white?
Others say we're always right!
Other people say the same things too,
They are just like me and you!

We are all just the same,
All of us should take the blame!
Other people say the same things too,
They are just like me and you!

Patrick Ferry (14)
Christian Brothers School, Belfast

Wasting Away

Sitting on the ground all alone
Hungry, homeless wanting a home.
I'm slowly slipping away
But no one cares, I'm just a stray.
I need help, I'm full of despair
But people walk past me without a care.
A lack of food makes me weak
I now realise I have no hope
My outlook's bleak.

Leah Kelly (14)
Dundonald High School, Dundonald

Madness

The youth of the nation
Brainwashed by the big screen
The glamorisation of war is sickening
Conditions are obscene

Limbs lie severed on the streets paved with blood
Along with the rubble
Made from homes of innocent children
Who now lie dead.

Civilians lie shell-shocked
As the explosions drop to destroy
Anything in their path
The iron giants rumble off into the horizon
To cause more destruction.

Millions of pounds are spent destroying people and cities
Millions are spent saving them.

Kurtis Davidson (14)
Dundonald High School, Dundonald

Wars

All I could hear around me were bombs and explosions, people
                                                with shell shock.
I could see blown up pieces of cars, legs, arms and blood everywhere,
It smelt like a barbeque with smoky burnt rotting flesh
                                                with petrol fumes.
All I could feel was pain, as if I was thrown into a furnace,
There were people running around screaming in pain and fright.
There were people with their legs and arms blown off
                                                with blood everywhere.
There were men running around with guns, firing them
                                                at innocent civilians.

Lee Welsh (14)
Dundonald High School, Dundonald

War

The smell of rotting flesh from the dead bodies as I hear the bombs
                                                                going off
Clinging to my gun and friends, looking at a building
The smell of the flowers in the field and the horrible smell of fear
All I can hear is shouting and bullets firing, frightened out of my boots
The sound of all the guns and artillery as I have my head buried
                                                                in the sand
You really don't know what you have got until you've lost it!

John Nelson (14)
Dundonald High School, Dundonald

Poverty

I feel desolate inside this hopeless body.
I plead for a chance in life to feel I have a proper place.
This world is cruel to us, alone in this land of hopeless friends.
Families torn apart by the natural cruelty in this awful world.
The smell of my friends, decaying beneath the rubble of what
                                                        was once my home.
Every time I turn around the people are always there
Their faces haunt me and their screams echo in my brain.

Lauren Wilson (14)
Dundonald High School, Dundonald

Nothing

Nothing else to see but death
Noting else to smell but decay
Nothing else to hear but screams of pain and terror
Nothing else to taste except dust and charcoal in the air
Nothing else to feel except fear, sadness and loneliness
No one will do anything about it so there's nothing else to do
                                                        but pray . . .

Bobbi Porte (14)
Dundonald High School, Dundonald

War

The civilians of the world were at risk, war was in place.
The destruction began as the rubble of the houses came
crashing down.
The limbs flying everywhere, I could taste the sick coming up my throat
I felt the shrapnel of the bullets as I picked them up.
I couldn't believe the stench of the rotting bodies as we marched
past them
The smell of the vile aroma of decay.
From a distance, I could see the destruction, as the guns were blazing,
Leaving a trail as they moved on to their next destination.

Aaron Graham (14)
Dundonald High School, Dundonald

War

Bodies flying everywhere dead and unmoving
People running from the guns that never stop
The soldiers that fight will never come home
They are fighting a war without meaning.

Clarke Burns (14)
Dundonald High School, Dundonald

Forest

F orests will not be here forever
O ur selfishness is destroying them quicker
R unning free through the trees
E verything in the forest will be lost
S omething needs to be done fast
T he trees need your help.

Alice Hamilton (13)
Glenlola Collegiate School, Bangor

Homeless

My own home,
My comfy bed,
Just a place to rest my head.
All gone in a day,
Couldn't afford to pay,
Felt like I'd rather just be dead.

On my mate's floor,
Knocking on some folk's doors,
Not knowing where to head,
Every day's a chore,
I really just wish for more,
But now the pavement is my bed.

Scrounging for food,
Never in a good mood,
I just want to be fed.
I'm misunderstood,
I'd pay if I could,
But now my life's full of dread.

Once the good times flowed,
Now I've no fixed abode,
All I see is the red.
So you just sleep in your cosy bed,
Your nice warm place to rest your head,
I'll still be here in the morning,
Take this as your advanced warning.

Belinda Cree (14)
Glenlola Collegiate School, Bangor

The Homeless Girl

I walk along the street all warm in my coat
But still I can feel the cold at my throat.
A girl stands there; she's looking at me,
I think and I wonder who could she be?
I see her there, she's all alone,
She's not like me, she has no home.

The homeless I thought were so far away
But here she is beside me today.
Look at her clothes, so tattered and torn
The cold must jag her like a sharp thorn.

I think so hard of what I could give
Just so this one young girl may live
In warmth, with happiness and love,
So she may have peace like a dove.

I call her over and take her home
Tonight there will be no more streets to roam.
Now she is home with my sister and me
She is now part of my family.

I walk along the street all warm in my coat
But still I feel the cold at my throat.
A girl stands there, she's looking at me
I think and I wonder where would she be?
If I had left her all alone
If I hadn't brought her home.

Emma McKee (14)
Glenlola Collegiate School, Bangor

Full Of NRG

Climate change is out and about
There is no doubt we'll go out like a light.
Scorching temperatures, freezing nights
You can see it happening at any height.

Greenhouse gases we learn in classes
Renewable energy, carbon footprint you can help
Going green, make a scene!
Renew your energy, solar panels, turbines
Walk! Driving releases CO_2 gases.

You can do these things and make a difference
Animals will have a home
Polar bears will still be known
Life will live longer
People become stronger
Don't be greedy because you're needy!

Jessica McKee (14)
Glenlola Collegiate School, Bangor

World Hunger

W omen, men and children are eating obsessively
O besity is becoming an epidemic
R apid growth in wasting food unnecessarily
L aborious diets that make you like a stick
D eserving people need your help

H unger kills eighteen thousand children every day
U nderdeveloped water systems kill
N utrition, what's that? You hear them say
G iving them scurvy and making them severely ill
E nergetic children are nowhere to be seen
R emember this when you aren't lean.

Ciara Mallon (14)
Glenlola Collegiate School, Bangor

From The City To The Town

I once lived in Belfast, a people kind of town
A cocktail-covered street with yella, black 'n' brown.
I'm not a racist and colour's kinda cool
When ya milk bottle-white like me ya rule.
When I came to Bangor, colour's kinda rare,
It's like most of you from Dublin are freckled and fair.
But I know there's them that thinks, if you're black you're mingin',
Unless you're in the charts and it's garage you are singin'.
I've a mate who's Egyptian and hence
His neighbours call him names cos they haven't got the sense.
You see, you see, cos unlike me,
They paid no attention in their geography.
Hope you follow this, it's rap that I'm singin'
And it's all you damn fool racists that are mingin'.
You see, you see, just like me,
Appreciate the culture they're givin' it free.
We get everything first in the city
It takes a while to filter to the country, it's a pity
But smell the coffee people, take a look around
You're the minority, half the world is brown!

Katie Glenn (14)
Glenlola Collegiate School, Bangor

Pollution

P ollution
O nly people are to blame
L ots of trees and oceans being ruined
L ives of animals at risk
U psets Mother Nature
T rees being damaged
I t makes the air very dirty
O zone layer is becoming thinner
N asty dirt in the air.

Lauran Brown (14)
Glenlola Collegiate School, Bangor

Planet Earth

Planet Earth can be saved
Saved from all the war
Saved from all the poverty
And saved from all the horror.

Young children going to war
What are they fighting for?
A chance to live, a chance to die?
All we hear is a rallying cry.

Planet Earth can be saved
Saved from all the hate
Saved from all the wrong
And saved from all debate.

Disaster zones in peril
No one can hear their scream
Dictators ruling their lives
Freedom is a dream.

Planet Earth can be saved
Saved from all destruction
Saved from the climate change
And saved from all corruption.

The weather is warm, now it's cold
The weather men are getting old
Climate change is on its way
It will rain another day.

Planet Earth can be saved
Saved from deforestation
Saved from all the acid rain
And saved from altercation

Trees so green and all in bloom
Cut down just to make some room
Infertile ground lies for years
The animals can't see our tears

Planet Earth can be saved
Saved by me and you
Saved by everyone around
Will *you* join in too?

Hannah McNamara (14)
Glenlola Collegiate School, Bangor

I Give You Trees

I give you trees
I give you bees
I give you apples, pears and grizzly bears
But what do you give me?

My atmosphere, it is quite clear, is being destroyed by *you!*
To all those cars and TVs you use, it is due.
My resources are few and far between
All I have is just one dream -
To be clean!
So spare a thought for me
Next time you jump in the sea or climb a tree
Don't drive, try to cycle
Don't waste time and just recycle.
Don't refuse to reuse
For me your one and only planet Earth
It's my due.

Hannah Lindsay (14)
Glenlola Collegiate School, Bangor

Racism

If we were birds, where would we be?
Open your eyes, maybe then you will see.
There are black birds, blue birds, yellow birds and red,
White birds, green birds, brown birds instead.

Humans are black, brown, yellow, red and white,
What does it matter? Yet we still fight!
We all have the same organs, lungs, kidneys and a heart
All of God's fine work of art.

Turn us inside out, we will all look the same
Maybe then there would be no nasty comments and no sly games.
So if we were birds, where would we be?
Open your eyes, maybe then you will see.

Children and adults bullied every day
Because they look and act in their own way.
Just think if that were you,
You would feel hurt, depressed and lonely too.

Brittany Smyth (14)
Glenlola Collegiate School, Bangor

Racism

R eligion, colour, gender, age differences in these can lead to rage
A ll people are the same inside but some make fun of those different
on the outside
C alling names and making fun or even worse, fighting, killing
and making them run
I n the name of God, man can't you see, that they're all exactly
like you and me
S o what we need to do is
M ake the world equal for you and for me.

Laura Edwards (14)
Glenlola Collegiate School, Bangor

Young Writers - A World of Difference Northern Ireland

Busy Buzzy Bees

Buzz, buzz, buzz,
What's with all the fuss?
Oh, it's a bee
The producers of honey
They make lots of money.
Yellow and black stripes
There are different types
Even though some sting
Bees are important for pollinating.

Soon they won't be able to live here anymore
Some choose to ignore -
They think bees are a distraction
But most are taking action
Against their extinction.
They are on the endangered list
So we must learn to co-exist
Or else it'll be an environmental disaster -
All plants will surely diminish faster.

Sarah Cheung (14)
Glenlola Collegiate School, Bangor

A Hunger For Love

Longing, hoping, waiting
For the slightest glimmer of hope.
You can't deny the hunger in their eyes;
A hunger for love.
It's easy to despair
When the future is only for others.
You can't deny the hunger in their eyes;
A hunger for love.
These children beg for the things we throw out
Sobbing and cries are the echoing, resounding sound.
You can't deny the hunger in their eyes;
A hunger for love.

Hannah Bulmer (14)
Glenlola Collegiate School, Bangor

Recycling

If we recycle
We will keep the Earth clean
The trees so tall and the grass so green
So let's help the Earth
And see what it is worth.

Think of all the stuff we waste
Food, clothes and even toothpaste
Give all your old clothes to family or charity
Don't throw them in the bin
And you will be helping lots of children.

When you go to the shopping centre
Before you enter think what you are going to buy
We buy a lot of things we don't need
And do you know what I think . . . ?
It is pure greed!

Amanda Huston (14)
Glenlola Collegiate School, Bangor

Trees

I took a walk in the park today
And realised something odd
The lush green trees that once surrounded me
Had somehow disappeared.
I wondered and wondered where they had gone
When suddenly it hit me!
These trees that were gone
Had been cut down for me
Cut down for everybody!
Those lush green trees had been made into paper
Which I use every day
Then I realised I used it for nothing
I just threw it away.
But then I thought was it really worth it?
No! I'd rather have the trees.

Jennifer Storey (14)
Glenlola Collegiate School, Bangor

A Polar Bear's Plea

The ice is melting
I'm getting warmer
The ice is melting
I'll be here no longer
The ice is melting
I'm falling through
The ice is melting
I need help from you!

Turn off your light
You know it's right
Turn off your PC
It really helps me
Walk to school
It's so cool
If it's not far
Don't use the car!

If you do this
You'll help the Earth too
You'll see me in the wild
And not in a zoo!

Emma Coey (14)
Glenlola Collegiate School, Bangor

Animals And Extinction

Animals are becoming extinct
And they don't really like it
They might rebel against us humans
To see how we like it!

Animals are going to die
Thanks to us humans
And they should rebel because
Animals are really quite handy!

Judith Aitcheson (14)
Glenlola Collegiate School, Bangor

Dolphin Dreams

Dolphin
I am a dolphin leaping for joy
Diving here and there without a care
I feel free, gentle and light
Happily I talk and play all day.

Born to jump over the glittering sky
With the sun above sparkling over the water
The glistening waves come thrashing towards me
As I swim away my dreams come true
The feeling of being unstoppable crosses my mind.

My life is not all happiness
There is an element of danger in my life
Pollution in the ocean makes my life a misery
Fishing, well, I almost got caught in the nets
The threats are huge to me.

Please stop so I can live my life to the full.

Rebecca McDowell (14)
Glenlola Collegiate School, Bangor

Every Little Helps

Red pandas, I know a lot about
But really soon because of us, they're gonna get kicked out.
Well, where can I start, there's quite a lot to say
No time for us to wait until another day.

Red fluffy fur, oh how can we be cruel?
Endangered as we know, they're runnin' outta fuel.
Destroying their habitat, hunting them too
We need to help them, oh what can we do?

I'll tell you what, stop and have a little thought!
Turn off your lights in summer, it's too bright,
Be quick in the shower, way less than an hour.
When not too far, don't use the car
Turn off your TV
And help everybody.
It's destroying the Earth, can't you see?

Tammy Cosgrove (14)
Glenlola Collegiate School, Bangor

Poverty

Do you leave food on your plate?
Do you wish you didn't have to go to school?
Do you take clean water for granted?

Well, let me tell you something,
Many babies, children, teenagers, adults and elderly people
Would love to have any sort of food on their plates every night.

Not many children go to school in Third World countries
The truth is that in some poor towns there is not even one school
When in some of our towns there are maybe two or three.
In some Third World countries clean water is very hard to get,
Many men, women and children have to walk miles just to get
clean water
When all we have to do is turn on the tap.
One third of deaths are due to poverty, hunger and dehydration,
So what can you do to help?
You could start by sponsoring a child or donating money to charity
So don't just stand there and let poverty get worse,
You can make a difference to this worldwide problem.

Naomi Ellis (14)
Glenlola Collegiate School, Bangor

If Only They'd Think

Wiped out rainforests, habitats lost
The materials sold at such a high cost
Not just in money, also in effect
Yeah, the usual suspects
Those humans these days
They'll do whatever to be paid
Without a care in the world, cutting down our homes
I'm starting to become more alone
My friends are dying out, we're becoming extinct
If only they would stop and think.

Jessica Matear (14)
Glenlola Collegiate School, Bangor

Black And White

Black and white, it's only different through sight,
Black and white, it's only different with spite.

There are two big clouds over the world
One black and one white,
Some people say one is good, the other bad
Which makes other people so sad.

Black and white, it's only different through sight,
Black and white, it's only different with spite.

You should learn to think in terms of grey
A larger array
A mix of black and white
People with different skin
And less hatred and spite.

Treat everybody equally
Not violent and horrifically
Black and white, it's only different through sight
Black and white, it's only different with spite.

Sarah McVeagh (14)
Glenlola Collegiate School, Bangor

Litter

Litter is all along the streets
Pick it up; it's by your feet.
Put your wrappers in the bin
You wouldn't do it at home, that would be a sin.
Think about your world today
Or the government will have to pay.
Less money for schools and health
It's using up our country's wealth.
So take a minute to stop and stare
Pick up your litter, do you even care?

Bronagh O'Loan (12)
Glenlola Collegiate School, Bangor

The Blue Wizard In My Garden

There's a wizard at the bottom of my garden
Who lives in a big blue box
Mummy tells me all about him
So I know exactly what he likes.
I simply keep him well fed
He gets very hungry you know
But he doesn't eat crisps or sweeties like me
No, no, no, not my blue wizard
He likes Daddy's newspapers
Or Mummy's egg boxes
Or even my juice cartons
We have a deal, Wizard and I
I feed him our household waste
And he passes them on to someone who makes
Pencils, pens, notebooks, rulers
Cardboard boxes to play in
And sometimes even plastic bottles
We have a good deal Wizard and I
Maybe you should get a wizard
For the bottom of your garden
Maybe he'll even give you homemade pencils
If you're lucky!

Verity McDonald (15)
Glenlola Collegiate School, Bangor

A Chance For Change

Every spring of every year
A giant hole will appear
Where? you may ask.
Well, let me say
Over Antarctica
It's the size of the USA!

The weather is changing
From the way we know it
And you never know what's coming
Earthquakes, cyclones, hurricanes too
And these are just a few!

Cutting down forests
Cutting down trees
Destroying habitats
Just for our needs!

Just think of all the resources we waste
Throwing things out in all our haste
Think of the Earth and save your time
Reduce, reuse, recycle.

Lauren McGarvey (14)
Glenlola Collegiate School, Bangor

Save The Rainforest

Swinging through the trees
I felt a lovely breeze
But then I heard a crack
It was a lumberjack
Cutting down the trees
Right below my knees
Now I have no home
I feel so alone.

I am swinging very fast
I don't think I can last
The bright burning fire
My arms begin to tire
I finally get out
And I begin to shout
Now I have no home
I feel so alone.

Bang, bang! I can hear the gun
Bang, bang! I begin to run
Bang, bang! I find a bushy tree
Bang, bang! I hope he can't see me
Bang, bang! They shoot my chin
Bang, bang! They have got my skin
Bang, bang! All my pain is gone
And I will never see another dawn.

Stop cutting down trees
There are lots of stories like these
Of poor little chimps
That get killed, bad little imps
And set fire to their homes
Go and hear the groans
Please help us
And make a big fuss!

Elizabeth Crawford (14)
Glenlola Collegiate School, Bangor

Endangered Crocodiles

You may own my friend
As a handbag
Or a trend.

You may own my mum
As some trousers
On your bum.

If you like the look of leather
You're at the end of my tether
The purse that you own
Was from the skin on my bone.

Why would you want to?
What made you do it?
Wearing leather for fashion
It can't be a passion.

We used to live
So quiet and in peace
But now come the poachers
And they just won't cease.

Soon you won't see us
Except in the zoo
Your children won't have heard of us
To them we'll just be new.

Our skin is worth its weight in gold
How can people be that bold?

We aren't the cutest
You'll probably know
But give us a break
It's more than we can take.

Ten million of us
Are killed each year
For the sake of leather
Extinction we are near.

Sarah McBride (14)
Glenlola Collegiate School, Bangor

I Rushed Out Of My House Today

I rushed out of my house today, I hadn't any time
To turn out all my kitchen lights, I know it is a crime.
I didn't think about those people who really pay the price
But then a kind old friend of mine gave me some advice.

All that soot and steam and smoke
It's becoming the Earth's cloak.
The sun's beams get in but then can't escape
This heat is more than our Earth can take.

There's flooding in Spain
France has acid rain
There's a hurricane in Asia
And tsunamis in Malaysia.

Our trees get chopped down
To make way for a town
More factories are built
So our flowers start to wilt.

Our world is being destroyed
But it's a disaster we can avoid
If we all pull together
We can stop this bad weather.

So the next time you rush to go out
It's our world you should be thinking about
So turn off that light
To stop the Earth's plight
For our children and their children's children.

Holly Campbell (14)
Glenlola Collegiate School, Bangor

Homeless

I'm tired
I got fired.
How silly of me
Now I have no money!
I'm on my own
The other day I fell and broke my leg bone.
I can hardly walk
I'm only wearing one sock.

I get my food from a bin
Last night's dinner was from an old soup tin.
I slept under a tree
Oh how I miss my TV.

I've got no pillow or blanket
I'm now a pickpocket.
I don't like my life
I even lost my wife.

There is a homeless shelter near here
I've been there often as I've been homeless for nearly a year.
People could help the homeless by giving us food
It would really help raise our mood.

I wish people would see me as a human being
Instead of always assuming
I have feelings you know
Even if I do have to sleep outside in the snow.

Amy Mornin (14)
Glenlola Collegiate School, Bangor

Racism

Is it because I'm black?
Is it because I'm white?
It is not right to pick such a fight
The colour of my skin
Doesn't mean anything.
We're all the same
Let's not play that nasty game.

My religion, my culture or my race
Is a serious case
But just treat me equally
No need to act so cheekily
Be a good friend
And make amends.

It is illegal to treat me with no respect
So you will pay the price
Always treat me very nice
Violence, insults and threats
Is this the way you treat your pets?

Together, let's end all this pain
And forget all of the shame.
So cast off your prejudice
And replace hate with love
Let's make our skin colour something to be proud of.

Lucia Devon (14)
Glenlola Collegiate School, Bangor

A Radical Fight

They come in all colours and sizes
And through this a problem arises
It's racism!
They may speak a language
That we do not speak,
They may have a religion
That we find unique.

But why does it matter
Why do we care?
Would you be treated different
If the skin wasn't there?

So black is black
And white is white,
Why is life such a fight?
We are all the same
No matter what
So replace your thoughts
With those that we have got.
And remember we are who we are
And it's the man above
Who has the power.

Caroline Chambers (14)
Glenlola Collegiate School, Bangor

I Am A Turtle

I am a turtle
And my name is Myrtle.
My mum got caught in a net
And they told me they wanted a pet.
She never came home
And left me on my own.
I am a turtle all alone
And I lost my mother Joan.

I am a turtle
And my name is Myrtle.
As we are swimming in a group
We get caught and made into turtle soup.
Sometimes our shells are sold
To people that are quite bold.
I am a turtle all alone
And I might not live until I am fully grown.

I am a turtle
And my name is Myrtle.
Some of my sisters
Never got to meet their misters
As they got killed on the beach
When they were smaller than a peach.
I am a turtle all alone
Don't just think of this as a groan.

I am a turtle
And my name is Myrtle.
Soon we all could be dead
Not just gone to bed
We need to save our kind
So please keep that in mind.

Stop dumping trash
It does not take cash
Careful when at the beach
Not to stand on a turtle the size of a peach.
When using fishing nets
Make sure you don't catch any unwanted pets.

Please keep this in mind
We are running out of time.

Becky McCready (14)
Glenlola Collegiate School, Bangor

Litter, Litter!

Litter, litter all around
Litter, litter on the ground.
Why not put it in the bin?
It would only take a min!

Litter, litter on the street,
Litter, litter stuck on your feet.
Why not just pick it up?
It may only be a plastic cup.

Litter, litter is so bad
Litter, litter makes me mad.
Why do people think it's OK?
My opinion is no way!

Litter, litter just don't do it
Litter, litter have some wit.
If everyone stops it now
There will no longer be this row!

Anna Thompson (14)
Glenlola Collegiate School, Bangor

An Explanation For My Four-Year-Old Sister

In this world
There are some things
Some things
That cannot laugh or sing.

These things are sad
Because of you
They want to know
If you're sad too.

'But what have I done?'
I hear you ask.
These things
Have not yet been unmasked.

These things are children
Just like you
Except they're sad
And hungry too.

These children live so far away
They would not
Could not
Come to play.

These children are thirsty
Tired and hot
Unlike to you
A drink means a lot.

So when you go to throw
Some food away
Think to yourself
And even say,

'I have lots of food
Even some ham
I just don't realise
How lucky I am!'

These children
Who have less than me
Would give everything
Just to eat my tea.

So don't waste food
Or water too
These things are children
Just like you!

Lois Wheatland (14)
Glenlola Collegiate School, Bangor

Alone

I lie alone on the cold streets
With no family, no friends
And nothing to eat.

I lie here praying
For someone to come
To love me and care
And bring me home.

My clothes are torn
My knees are grazed
I'm beginning to wish
I was never raised.

I look at the people
Slowly walking past
They begin to see
I'm not going to last.

I shiver with cold
And curl into a ball
I think to myself,
This is my all.

Olivia McIntyre (13)
Glenlola Collegiate School, Bangor

Dream

How do you think I feel not to have a home?
Not able to go home or even use the phone.
Not to have anyone to go home to at night
Or have them tell me to sleep tight.
Now I have nowhere to live but under a tree
Where my only neighbour and best friend is a flea.
But maybe things will not always be this bad
Maybe I will not always be this sad.
Some day I will get away from this street
Or someone might give me something to eat
But for now this is only a dream.

Holly Milne (13)
Glenlola Collegiate School, Bangor

Litter

Litter is a crime
Prepare to pay the fine.
Better still, stop it at once!
Not just in a couple of months.

Claire Smyth (13)
Glenlola Collegiate School, Bangor

Tomorrow's Day

The sky a smoke screen
Rivers a slurry of death
The way it will be.

Charlotte McBride (13)
Glenlola Collegiate School, Bangor

Litter

Litter, litter all around
In the sea and on the ground
Plastic bags and metal tins
Recycle them, put them in the bins
Don't throw them away
It will come back on you someday!

Nicole Kinder (13)
Glenlola Collegiate School, Bangor

Mother Earth's Despair

As the sun burns in the sky
Mother Earth lets out a cry.
'Enough, enough, I've had enough,
This strain on me is far too tough!
This world I nurtured oh so well
Has gone from Heaven into Hell.
I'm far too warm from this global heat
Because of coal, oil, gas and peat.

As for the rainforest it makes me frown
To see my beautiful garden being cut down.
Cars and lorries give out smoke
The poisonous fumes make me choke.
Countries drown in their polluted lake
I get shaken up and the Earth does quake.
I feel like screaming, they call it a volcano
You may blame me but I'm only trying to show
That if we don't do something soon
I'll almost certainly go *kaboom!*
I need some support and a helping hand
We have the power to change, so let's see if we can!'

Zoë Purvis (14)
Limavady Grammar School, Limavady

Planet Earth Can Be Saved!

Next time you travel by car, stop and think
This can lead to endangered animals becoming extinct.
The water levels will probably rise,
This should not be too big a surprise!

The Earth is getting warmer due to global warming
The ice caps are deforming.
Coal, oil, gas and peat
Are all reasons for this heat.

The Earth can be saved though
Although the progress will be slow.
If we all join together
We can make things better.

As plants and animals are dying away
There is just one thing I need to say
Please help save the Earth and everything in it
Then the end of the tunnel might be lit!

Laura McLaughlin (13)
Limavady Grammar School, Limavady

Litter, Litter

Litter, litter is a crime
Pick it up or pay a fine.
Litter, litter is so bad
Why people do it, it makes me sad.

Litter, litter is not nice
If we don't stop it, it'll attract the mice.
Litter, litter that's why I write this song
But people still do it all day long.

Litter, litter we must stop it
We should all stop the habit.
Litter, litter is a crime
Pick it up or pay a fine!

John McCready (14)
Limavady Grammar School, Limavady

I Am A Lion

I am a lion of the vast open plain
I am asking you to listen and not refrain
So I can tell you the complete truth
That you are neglecting the world like a rotting tooth.

The rubbish you throw away in the bin
We all know it ends up in a swim.
In the vast open ocean today
You know sometime you will have to pay.

Fossil fuels are used everywhere
Keep on using them - you'll create a nightmare.
Up till now we have been alright
But now it's all not quite right.

Times have been bad and we've got through
But now hope's slim so we are coming for you.
Can you believe time's running out
So why, oh why, are you standing about?

Karen Jones (14)
Limavady Grammar School, Limavady

Animals

We are animals, big and small
We aren't afraid of humans tall.
In the trees is where we stay
And you selfish people you will pay.
For every time you chop a tree
You don't see what we see.
We lose our homes and all our things
And have to strain our precious wings
Flying up in the sky
Just to find a place to lie.
Every time we look around
We see litter on the ground
So please just take a minute
To stop, think and maybe bin it.

Niamh Fenlon (14)
Limavady Grammar School, Limavady

Beauty That Once Shone

I'm the mighty panda, hear me roar
This bamboo tree, what do you think it's for.
It's a great plant to eat
And you can use it as a fan in the intensive heat.

I'm the amazing bird, look at me fly
As I fly away in winter I wave you goodbye.
We go away in winter to try and get a tan
I've got to tell you a story about my best friend Dan.
Dan came home during the month of May
I'm telling you now, it wasn't a good day.
He came back home, the house was knocked down
He just looked at me and gave me a big frown.

I'm the mighty killer whale, watch me swim
Watch Free Willy, I was great in that film.
My ocean is getting destroyed I'm not that glad
People think it's nothing but it's actually really bad.
Before you know it, everything will be gone
And to think of the beauty that once shone.

Bosco McAuley (14)
Limavady Grammar School, Limavady

Blue

Plastic, glass and tin are all made for the blue bin.
There's white glass and brown glass and even green
The bottles are taken then scrubbed and cleaned.
The streets are filled with broken glass; it seems a hard
                                        and difficult task.
But all you need is one blue bin, it's as easy as this, put it all in!
There's always a bin not far from sight, so why drop it, try to fight
The temptation to throw it and leave it to fly
Put it in the bin and at least you've tried to save the world from litter,
                                        it's an easy thing.

Ryan Archibald (14)
Limavady Grammar School, Limavady

Cruel Fate

A troop of men walking to the hands of fate
Tearing out their dampened souls
Marching to the terminal gate.

God acts in cruel ways, rising above the minds of men
Watching lives fall apart
Waiting for the chosen ten.

Wondering what is to become of their life
Waiting,
Battling their internal strife.

Men act in cruel ways, rising above the mind of a child
Watching their lives fall apart
Fighting for the undignified side.

Melissa Duffy (14)
Limavady Grammar School, Limavady

Environment Poem

I know what to do in the future
From this day forward I will take it easy on the Earth.

Plant trees
Kill no living things
Help all creatures
I will restore the Earth where I am
Use no more of its resources than I need
So no more damage then is done
Prevent pollution from home
Recycle most things
Pick up litter.

I know what to do in the future
From this day forward just be kind to my world.

Christopher McElreavey (13)
Limavady Grammar School, Limavady

Poor Johnny

The bodies are being collected tonight again
Exactly what Johnny Logue had been saying,
'A man doesn't live too long out here
We all know that death is very near.'

Pity he didn't see his daughter be born
And give her the ring which he had worn.
He treasured his girl throughout his life
He told us repeatedly that she would make a great wife.

We found him alone, lying there still
Looking so meek, so pale, so ill.
We know he was shot once over the top
And poor Johnny Logue fell like a drop.

If only we could go back to when
We were children and only ten
'A man doesn't live too long out here
We all know that death is very near.'

Maria Duddy (14)
Limavady Grammar School, Limavady

Earth Can Still Be Saved

Everything was perfect
Not a thing was wrong
Planet Earth was a wonderful place
Until people came alone.

They came, they saw, they conquered,
Without a thought for Earth.
Polluting air and land and sea
Her state got worse and worse.

The Earth has suffered greatly
From the human raid
But if we treat her properly
Then Earth can still be saved.

If we start to consider
And start to act right now
We may make Earth much better
And save our world somehow.

John Fallows (14)
Limavady Grammar School, Limavady

The Army

I hear the sounds of the wolves
As they approach closer
I can hear them around my house
And I'm alone and afraid.

They howl through the dark night
To say they have found me
As I shiver in my bed
And their cold melody pierces the silent night.

I hear the sound of the planes flying overhead
Looking for me
Making sure I don't run away
From the approaching army.
I hear the sounds of the bombs landing outside
Lights flash outside as they land on the ground
And destroy the landscape around me
And the homes of the people I hold close.

The howls grow louder and I stay inside,
Afraid of what is happening outside
Afraid of the damage the army are causing
And afraid of the beasts that they use to instil fear into their victims.

The time passes slowly
And I hear the brutal sounds of the army coming closer
Preparing for their assault
And preparing to make the city explode.

Eventually the howls of the wolves die down
And the sounds of the planes fade away into nothing
And the marching of the army begins to quieten
And I decide to look outside to see the damage.

As I emerge from my house,
Other people around me are doing the same
We look around at the devastation before our eyes
And the rubble that was once our town.

I can see the hurricane dying in the distance
And its army and beasts die with it
The howling and engines of planes die,
As the wind becomes nothing but a gentle breeze
And the army has faded into a flood of water up to our knees,
The army of water that we were so afraid of.

Amy Brussard (15)
North Coast Integrated College, Coleraine

The Thunder And The Lightning Song

The sun doesn't tarry long today
It hides, taking refuge behind fluffy balls of grey.
The world turns dark before it's night
As the world stands in suspended motion.
The clouds await their distant call
In order to begin the downpour;
They do not wait long before a faint rumble is heard
The clouds prepare, loosening their load
And there it is the flash of light.
The sun hides further as in night
Fearing its fatal foes while
The clouds wearily drop their loads
Hurtling, splashing to below.

Plop!
A man looks up as the first splash reaches his back
Trickling down his back, cooling his burning skin.
He raises his arm as the procession proceeds
Relieving in the sudden cool
The sudden breeze.
He gently bends to pick his load
Heading on the road
Knowing now is the time to head indoors before the lightning finds a host.
He heads in, flicking switches from on to off,
He would not be one to be burnt from the lightning's wrath.
He snuggles into a chair listening to the storm's ongoing calls
And surely soon he rests his weary head
While thunder and lightning continue overhead.

Another deafening roar makes them huddle closer
A blinding flash of light illuminates the darkened sky
Where has this beast come from?
Why isn't anyone there to shelter them?
The children watch the other's faces fearfully
As they turn white in the bright light.
Roar! goes the monster again
But where is it, where does it hide?

Surely a mighty beast would not hide its huge mass,
Its shadow darkens the sky but where, oh where does it hide?
'Mummy, will soon be here,'
Whispers one trying to still fear.

And on and on the torrent goes
Ignoring those far below
Not ceasing for the cheerful greetings
Or the children's gentle pleadings.
The thunder gives a mighty roar
And the lightning answers with its lightning call.
The thunder groans on and on
While the lightning shrieks its angry song.

Christine Cartwright (15)
North Coast Integrated College, Coleraine

The Storm

Uneasy silence.
The sun flees from the dark clouds
That take its place
Polluting the sky.
The Earth holds its breath
In nervous anticipation
Of what is to come.

Deafening noise.
Raindrops shoot down
Like a million shooting stars
Glad to be free
Bouncing against the ground
Before leaping up again
Gurgling in delight.
The angry wind howls through the air
Its screams piercing the night like a dagger.
Delicate flowers cower at the attack
And hang their pretty heads, drowning.
The old trees raise their branches in protest
But the wind shows no mercy.
It spins around and around
Pushing and pulling and tugging
Until the magnificent trees can stand no longer
And fall to the ground,
Their dying groans lost in the chaos.

Quiet weeping.
Tiny children pull the blanket tighter round them
Seeking comfort where none can be found.
Time trudging by so slow, so slow,
Hands over ears trying to stop
The pounding rain marching along the rooftop
From ringing in their heads
Curled up small wishing the storm away
Wishing, wishing, wishing
and then . . .

Serene silence.

Emily Brussard (15)
North Coast Integrated College, Coleraine

Wars Go Wrong

There is one problem I would like to share
And that is war is everywhere.
The problem is it kills us all,
That the men die and the children cry
The war kills us all.

The wars can cause anyone their demise
The war goes on with enemy spies.
Why can't we have love, care and peace?
They want more land and nothing else,
I want love and harmony
But some people will never see.

Without the wars good friends we'd be
But then again, there will be fights
And we'd keep out of each other's sights.
Wars cannot be stopped unless we all agree to live in perfect harmony
Until that day more wars will be, someday, everyone will see,
Someday.

Adam Burke (12)
Omagh Academy, Omagh

Our Dark And Dusty World

Our world is like
A beautiful masterpiece smudged with ink
A house abandoned, no longer cared for
A beam of sunlight wiped from existence.

No longer do people know or even care what will happen
To this world as we know it, nor how much time is left.
Before our world is destroyed thanks to the darkest demon in our time
Eating away at the atmosphere ruining our rivers and seas
That every person in this world uses and takes for granted.

If people stopped to think of all the things
Mankind can do to reduce pollution, then maybe,
We might just be able to make a happy healthy planet
Out of this dark and dusty world.

Lindsay Hunter (12)
Omagh Academy, Omagh

Save Our World

This world will soon be gone
But no one knows how long
We have until the day will come
And everyone will run and run
Away from the well-known fact
We all need to begin and act.
To stop our world from disappearing
We need to make sure everyone's hearing
That we need to make a change
And choose from the worldwide range
Of things that anyone can do
We really need to get this through.

So stop cutting down our trees
You need to understand please, please!
If one person would stop and think
We might save just one little mink
But if everyone pulls in together
We may be saved from this forever!

Sarah Moore (12)
Omagh Academy, Omagh

Littering

Our streets used to be lovely and black
But now they're under litter attack.
The footpaths were a clear walking space
But on them now, we fall flat on our face.

Think before you throw it down
Or you will get a litterbug crown.
So put your rubbish in the bin
'Cause littering is a deadly sin.

Rachael Colhoun (12)
Omagh Academy, Omagh

War

Where is the love in this world today?
People are starting to go astray.
Killing people, dropping bombs
Every hour of the night and day

Where is the love in this world today?
Just think about people who aren't as lucky as us.
While we can get a ride on the bus
They have to walk and walk and walk!

Where is the love in this world today?
Soldiers getting killed for their countries
While their loved ones sit at home and worry.
Oh where is the love?

Bethany Kyle (12)
Omagh Academy, Omagh

The Environment

Look at our environment
So lush and green
And the sky so blue with a lovely sheen.

But this awful pollution
Is wrecking this land
So wake up people and stop this destruction
And making our land look bland.

But it is not just us who are suffering
It is our friends the animals who are suffering too.
The caps are melting so stop right now
Before we do our planet harm.

David Harpur & John Pak (12)
Omagh Academy, Omagh

Pollution

Pollution is happening
And it's getting worse every year
But it's really not fair
On the deer.
Pollution is happening
And it's getting worse every year
If we don't cut down
There will be a lot of smoke in the air.

Pollution is happening
And it's getting worse every year
We don't even think to stop
And learn what effect it's having on the atmosphere.
Pollution is happening
And it's getting worse every year.
What can we do?
A lot I hear!

David Long (12)
Omagh Academy, Omagh

Wars Come And Go

Wars come and go,
Wars here, wars there
Wars past, wars present, wars future.
Is it a fight for power, for glory, for revenge?
Well, here is what I can tell you,
Iraq is in chaos, people are dying and it's not very nice.
Cars are exploding, buildings collapsing and guns' triggers
                                            being pulled
But here's an idea on how we stop it.
We throw down our guns, say sorry, make friends
                          and share power together.
If we could do this, you have to admit, the world would all be better.

Jamie Rankin (12)
Omagh Academy, Omagh

Global Warning

The planet is slowly heating up
Don't try to disagree
You really can't ignore it,
You can't run away or flee.

There is no quick way to fix it
It's going to take some time
It's going to be an uphill fight
But an even harder climb.

It's not impossible - don't get me wrong
It may be hard, it may be long,
You may think that it's rather strange
But it's possible for you to reverse the change.

Walk instead of taking the car
Even if you are going far.
Recycle every day of every week
And the future will not be so bleak.

Global warming can be stopped
But we must do it together
So children can walk across the hills
And smile among the heather.

Ryan Watt (12)
Omagh Academy, Omagh

Dreaming Of Tomorrow

I'm dreaming of tomorrow
Where everyone is well
When a cure for all disease is found
No pain or suffering.

I'm dreaming of tomorrow
Where everyone is full
No searching through a trashcan
Or starving with no food.

I'm dreaming of tomorrow
Where everyone is proud
Not following what others do
Individuality is the key.

I'm dreaming of tomorrow
Where a child's life is safe
No hurting, tears or bullying
With a smile upon their face.

I'm dreaming of tomorrow
Where the world is eco-friendly
When we shrink our carbon footprint
Considering our future!

Lauren English (14)
Rathfriland High School, Rathfriland

The Big Green Issue

Global warming is it true
Or is it just talk by me and you?
Is it really melting the ice
Or is it just the roll of the dice?

Who made the carbon footprint, was it you
Or is it just the stuff of tales?
Is it just the big sports cars
Or is it people watching TV in bars?

Is it the planes in the sky
Why all the need to fly?
Is it the lorries on the road, the ones delivering our food?
Are they really doing good?

What is all the use in all this talk
If we don't get out and walk?
We should all take our bikes
And all go on a hike.

Eoin Dolan (12)
St Michael's College, Chanterhill

Poverty

It's so unfair
They do not care
About important things
Like world death and poverty.
All we need is some kind of key
A key to unlock a lock out of sight
It appears once in the stars at night
And through the lock we fail to see
A world without poverty.

Mark Mulligan (12)
St Michael's College, Chanterhill

Litter

Litter, litter everywhere
It really does give me a scare
And if we stay in this state
Then only time will decide our fate.

Don't throw it on the road
Put it in a bin or stay at home
And if it kills an animal
Then I would think that I'm in trouble!

But sure what can I do
'Cause this may cause the flu?
But according to the government
He has better things to do.

So please, please don't drop your litter
'Cause it really makes me flitter
And if you don't have a scare
The world will be a nightmare.

Christopher Flanagan (12)
St Michael's College, Chanterhill

Poverty Speaks

P icking coins off the street
O nly a few scraps to eat
V ery uncomfortably I have to sleep
E veryone ignores me, it's like I don't exist
R arely anyone stops to say hello
T oo cold to sleep, I want to go home
Y es, how I regret it now.

S leeping alone, no friends at all
P retending to be cool and have a ball
E ating scraps, never good food
A nd I'm always in a bad mood
K icks and blows I get at night
S top, why can't it stop?

Ruairí Doherty (14)
St Michael's College, Chanterhill

A Growing Problem

We are all letting our world go bad
It is making some people very mad
We should all recycle and our choices reserve
 Because we waste more stuff than we deserve.

Our waters are polluted and dirty
Our streets are full of litter
Our fossil fuels are wasting away
We should all start saving and stop wasting.

The ice is melting fast
The trees are falling down
If we do not stop this now
Our future will be extremely grim.

Everyone can do their bit
Just start recycling
Saving energy and oil
If we don't our beautiful world is going to spoil.

Eoín Baxter (12)
St Michael's College, Chanterhill

The Big Green Issue

Well I'm here to tell you to stop
We're not getting any cleaner
So soon the world's going to *pop!*

Littering, pollution, global warming
It's all starting to rise
So help out a bit everyone
Before even more animals die.

So you're asking
What's to be done?
I'm telling you now
Use your blue bins
And don't forget,
Reduce, reuse, recycle.

Ryan Carney (11)
St Michael's College, Chanterhill

Environmentally Friendly

To reduce your carbon footprint
There are some simple things to do,
Everyone could walk some more
And not waste so much fuel.

Don't throw your litter on the ground
Take the time to find a bin.
Simple things like this
Make this world better to live in.

We should grow more plants
Stop cutting down trees,
Paper is made from trees you know
So use your paper wisely please.

By doing all these things
There's so much damage we can prevent,
So all of us can do our bit
To help our environment.

Adam Breen (12)
St Michael's College, Chanterhill

Sadly Smoking

Lots of people start smoking
All of them end up choking.
It makes you smell
Everyone can tell.
Smoking costs too much
Such a waste
Stopping is good
Everyone should.
Smoking kills us all
Nobody walks tall
Doesn't matter if you smoke or not
Others smoke near you and hurt you too.

Jason Donnelly (12)
St Michael's College, Chanterhill

Young Writers - A World of Difference Northern Ireland

Stop And Think!

Stop and think
About the world
Will we sink?
Stop and think!

Stop and think
Whether the scientists know what they are talking about.
Or is this just a joke?
Stop and think!

Stop and think
About the weather.
Will we have sun or will we have snow?
Stop and think!

Stop and think
About the world.
Will it be here for your generation?
Stop and think!

James Britton (12)
St Michael's College, Chanterhill

The Environment

Litter, litter everywhere
All around us, even in our hair.
Litter, litter everywhere we go
We should limit our carbon footprint until it's quite low.
Global warming, is it true?
Some say yes, what about you?
Recycling or pollution
Only one of these can be the solution.
Rainforests are being cut
Right down to their last foot.
Smoke from industries dirties the air
Do you really care?

Domhnall Boyle (12)
St Michael's College, Chanterhill

A Way Of Life

His sleeping bag is cold and wet
His temporary home is set
He rests his head against the cobbled street
He has no supper or food to eat
Every person that passes by
Throws out a few coppers and makes a sigh
As if to say, 'Oh my, I hate you
Have you nothing else to do?'
But the answer is no, he doesn't
He has tried before but it's just hopeless
He'll cry himself to sleep every night
And think being homeless is a pretty dull life.

Patrick Dolan (14)
St Michael's College, Chanterhill

The Hole

Listen people! I have something to say.
We are destroying God's gift to us, what do you say?
Well, for one there's the hole in the ozone layer,
It's triple the size of Australia!
If you don't believe me then look at the Arctic.
Act now to live past twenty, who knows you might live to be ninety!

Jamie Antony Appleby (12)
St Michael's College, Chanterhill

Racism

R acist to us, they think we don't care
A nd after all, it's very unfair
C all us names and make fun of our colour
I now think I can't be bothered
S o please stand up against the mugs
M y life is ruined by these thugs.

Eddie Coutney (14)
St Michael's College, Chanterhill

Poverty

People are poor everywhere
But no one seems to care.
Why don't people share
To help people here and there?
Some live in bins
They've got no kin
And that is a sin.
So help me please
To stop this disease
That is poverty.

Jack O'Dolan (12)
St Michael's College, Chanterhill

Trees

Oh why do trees have to be cut down?
It makes everybody put on a frown.
Trees would like to help us breathe
If they weren't cut down I'd be relieved.
Slicing down trees ruins animals habitats
Putting them into zoos, less of that.
Burning trees just for fun
But then you'll see what consequences you've done.
Trees are definitely so cool
Do anything to them and you'll be a fool.

Tiernach O'Reilly (12)
St Michael's College, Chanterhill

Fading Away - Haiku

The iceberg so cold
Been on the Earth for so long
Now fading with heat.

Ciaran Monaghan (12)
St Michael's College, Chanterhill

The Witch

Sitting in the shade one day
Trying to write a poem,
It was sunny, warm, nice you'd say
Listening to trees groan.
Until she came like a storm
And said, 'You cannot stay!'
We huffed and puffed all we liked
But we couldn't get our way.
The witch we say, that's her name
It's people like her we all agree
That ruin our world today.
We look back, we shout, we cannot see
Our lovely peaceful trees.
Instead we see to our surprise
Dead grass, dead trees, dead bees!
We think and think and think alike
And something comes to mind
We will be green, we will not litter
To save all of mankind.

Kevin Caulfield (14)
St Michael's College, Chanterhill

Nature To Capitalise

I stood where our forests and trees once stood tall
Majestic and beautiful
But it's in our nature to capitalise
Why can't we just stop?
But the damage has been done
The smell of sweet wood is gone
Nothing but a ghost is remaining.
Surely there is another way
To feed this monstrous cause
Than destroying what was gifted to us
By our one and only leader.

Liam Cassidy (14)
St Michael's College, Chanterhill

Blame

Why put your rubbish on the road?
Sure it doesn't make much sense.
It's not going to turn to gold.
It's only going behind a fence.

It's not worth anything if
Others clean up after you,
You think you are a king,
But you belong in a zoo!

Some animals live on the roadside
You should think about others,
Some poor animal may die
And animals too have mothers.

Some poor bird may not coo
So please wise up.
Why don't you do something?
For you alone are to blame.

Ciaran Corrigan (12)
St Michael's College, Chanterhill

Grey World

Is it true what they say?
Do we have a part to play
In being green?

Cars burn fuel which chokes our air,
Fumes from power plants grimly stare
At those of us below.

Rubbish on our waterways
Factories create a haze of smoke.
Solar panels, can we try?
Thermal energy, we should buy.
Save our planet before we die!

James Allen (12)
St Michael's College, Chanterhill

What About Our World?

What about our world
All those dying rainforests?
Those poor plants and animals
Suffering because of us.

Don't get in that amazing Mustang
It's classy, it's cool but it's bad.
We put out bad gases into the air
And then we say it's not fair.

Don't throw that wrapper on the floor,
Don't dump that bottle in a ditch,
Please don't litter
Because if you taste it, it tastes so bitter.

So now you know
Don't ever do it.
You know it's bad
So don't do it lad.

Oisin Corrigan (12)
St Michael's College, Chanterhill

Think Of The Children And Save Our World

I've an urgent message, listen to what I say
Lose the car, take the bike today.
If we want to keep the trees lush and green
Make use of your recycling machine.
Earth is a wonderful place
The thought of its destruction is a disgrace.
Think of the penguins and the polar bear
Oh come on, you *have* to care!
You must be able to improve your ways, think of some!
Remember, it will affect what's to come!

Michael Cameron (12)
St Michael's College, Chanterhill

The Big Green Issue

Don't be mean, please be clean!
So much rubbish to be seen.
To me it's such a sin
Throw your rubbish in a bin!

Then there is pollution
So what's the solution?
When parents drive to school
They could choose to walk and save fuel.

Reduce, reuse, recycle
It's really quite simple.
Cartons go in blue
Wrappers go in the black, easy!

Global warming, is it true?
Heat, heat, phew
Land that's dry, land that's flooded
Tick-tock, unfair.

Jamie Farry (11)
St Michael's College, Chanterhill

The Big Green Issue

The world's major countries
Are the cause of global warming.
The factories just keep making their cars.
Help us save the world.

Rubbish gathers up
Greenhouse gases build.
That is why we should recycle and reuse.

Pollution is destroying the ozone layer.
If we cut down rubbish and pollution
We might be able to stop global warming.
So help me save the world.

Darragh Foy (12)
St Michael's College, Chanterhill

War

The world would be a better place, a better place today
If only, if only, peace would come to stay.
War is breaking out, anger is about
Lots of lives will be lost
All at a stupid silly cost.
Lots of soldiers will be sent far away to battle hard
In the end they may all end up in a dull graveyard.
Nobody yet knows what the outcome will be
But it's sure to be a horrific sight no one will want to see.
A young man leaves his family and friends,
Where is this going to end?
The barracks are wet, cold and dooming
With a hard day's battle and enemies looming.
Many a heart will be broken and torn
With hundreds of widows left to mourn.

Niall Carson (14)
St Michael's College, Chanterhill

The Big Green Issue

You can help
Just do your part
Help the environment
From losing its heart.

Littering's bad
Help it stop
Help the Earth
Tick and tock.

If you recycle
You can help the weather
Put paper in the blue bin
Forever and ever.

Kevin Fitzpatrick (12)
St Michael's College, Chanterhill

Pollution

We weren't allowed to play
Because it was raining all day.
It was really dirty rain
Falling down the pane.
When the dirty rain stopped
Ordinary rain dropped.
Spreading slurry are the farmers
It's what they do but are they harmers?

Barry Mulligan (12)
St Michael's College, Chanterhill

War

Gunshots are everywhere
Boom! go the bombs
There's scared children
Families are wrecked
Countries are always in a fight
This time it's
America versus Iraq.

Cormac Valentine (12)
St Michael's College, Chanterhill

The Sun

We watch it rise and set
We see what its vision of beauty brings
Life, beauty to the environment
There is one important thing it can give, the future.
We think as we sit next to our loved one
About love, marriage, a family
Even though it withers away in the distance
We think today is another day.

Oisin Clancy (14)
St Michael's College, Chanterhill

Extinction

All the animals trot along the stones
Not knowing that they will soon be bones.
All thanks to us they have no home
But let's make a difference by reading this poem.
While many people sit in a pub and drink
Do you ever take time to think
That while you may be committing a crime
The animals will soon run out of time?
Take the rhino for example, will it soon be too small to trample?
Many think it's OK to take their horns
But couldn't these poachers just eat some corn?

Rory Brennan (14)
St Michael's College, Chanterhill

The Game Of War

My teacher once said to me, 'War is coming boy, be ready for when
she strikes.'
My recruitment officer said, 'War is here son and she's calling for you.'
My commanding officer shouted at us, 'War is happening
and you're on the front line!'
My best buddy uttered his last words, 'War has taken my life,
don't let her destroy yours!'
The bombs dropped from the sky like raindrops, 'This is it boys,
make peace!'
Rescue teams rummaged through the rubble, 'They were young,
too young for war!'
The priest said at my funeral, 'War has taken his life but war still
ravages on.'
I heard that we won but in war there are no winners, everyone loses.

Paul Donaghey (14)
St Michael's College, Chanterhill

The Search

Pockets of our old worn coats empty
We lie in the deserted streets, cold and damp
Invisible, unwanted, a waste of space.
The dark street echoes our footsteps
As we continually walk aimlessly through the night
Not sure what we're looking for
Probably comfort, warmth, a life.

Eoghan Corrigan (14)
St Michael's College, Chanterhill

War

The sound of a gun is fun to none
Whilst young men wither and die in the warm Gulf sun
Fighting for oil and other silly things.
Oh will we ever see the barrel of oil decrease in price
Or will it continue to burn in the warm Gulf sun?
Will peace be upon us ever so soon?
Will we see ceasefire in the warm Gulf sun?
Will terrorism end our fun?
Or will terrorists finally put down their guns?

Conor Doherty (14)
St Michael's College, Chanterhill

War!

Little children dying on the street
Women crying as their husbands get beat
Gunfire can't be ignored, it's all around
A soldier gets shot; he goes hard to the ground.
Houses raided when they need not
Citizens told today you will get shot!
War scares me right to the bone
But it makes me happy to hear the gunfire is done.

Luke Collins (14)
St Michael's College, Chanterhill

Be Green

Pollution is disgusting, it's bringing the world to its knees,
Lots of people think they can do as they please.
Because of the Twin Towers, there is a holy war,
The Twin Towers horror killed many, the invasion killed more.
The world is warming up and it's Man's doing.
If we aren't careful the world will be similar to Bedlam.
So people stop fighting, help the world become clean,
Come on everybody, let's be green.

Cailéan Dolan (12)
St Michael's College, Chanterhill

The Sun

T he sun is bright
H e's in the sky
E nvironmentally sound

S uddenly people come along and mess the world about and
U ntil we wise up
N ever shall we see ice caps again no doubt.

Sean Allen (14)
St Michael's College, Chanterhill

Death

It follows every single human being, merely a shadow
                                        shrouded in darkness.
It is patient because it knows there is no denying
                                        our undeniable doom.
It is the fear in a person's voice.
It is the sad acceptance in an elderly person's voice.
It is the grief and sorrow of mourning.
It is everything and nothing, the absolute, it is death.

Neal Beirne (14)
St Michael's College, Chanterhill

The Environment

T he world is becoming a stranger place
H ouses are taking up all the space
E vergreens are being cut down

E ven to make a simple pound
N ext thing is all the pollution
V ery quickly we need a solution for
I f it's solved it shall be a revelation
R ecycling is the way to go
O r our resources will be low
N ever do we think of homelessness but
M any face this loneliness
E xtinction is what our animals face
N ot unless we protect their race
T his is true, so what will you do?

Niall Beggan (14)
St Michael's College, Chanterhill

The Hobo

Cold and unkempt
His eyes dim and grey
An outstretched hand
Begging for pay.
Withered from the wind
And looks of disgrace
He sits still like a statue
At his usual place
And every so often
A coin rattles his cup
And his sour face disappears.

Finn Corrigan (14)
St Michael's College, Chanterhill

Racism

We all feel the same
We all bleed the same
We all cry the same
We all laugh the same
We all love the same
We all are born the same
We all die the same
We all feel scared
But what scares us the most is the difference in the colour of our skin.

Keiron Bostle (14)
St Michael's College, Chanterhill

Disgraceful

The amount of paper we waste is such a disgrace
Burning fossil fuels is such a sin
You may as well put them in a bin
We throw them away so freely you'd think we were in a relay
There's only one possible answer, litter!

James Carroll (12)
St Michael's College, Chanterhill

Litter

Litter is lying everywhere
On the streets
But some don't care
There has to be an improvement
So do your bit and look after the environment
Put your rubbish in the bin
After all, littering is a sin.

Connor O'Neill (12)
St Patrick's Academy, Dungannon

I Wish

I wish that people could see
What the world could be
If there was a stop to pollution
Extinction and poverty.

So listen mate, it isn't so great
Resting your head against the gate
The flowerbed, where you rest your head
The green, green grass, the mattress of your bed.

Pollution is not the best solution
To make the world a better place
'Cause if you pollute, what you are doing
Is making lots of dirtier space!

Are you interested in animals?
Protecting the endangered kinds?
Well, if you are just remember the next few rules in mind,
Recycle, ride your bicycle, leave your car at home, do not litter!
So would you consider protecting the endangered kinds?

Claire Mackle (12)
St Patrick's Academy, Dungannon

Please Come Home!

No food, no shelter,
No family or friends,
Homeless people surely want this to end.

A loving home, a roof over their head
Some food, some fun and even a bed!

We need to take action, we don't like this way
It can't keep happening day after day.
This might have happened because of family problems
Or maybe you're just sad,
But you are all breaking the nation's heart,
So come home, it's not all that bad!

Eimear Crealey (12)
St Patrick's Academy, Dungannon

The Homeless

I think it is wrong that there is nothing more being done to help
                                              the homeless
Some homeless people at one time had good jobs and a good home
But for whatever reason are now living on the streets.
I think there should be more places open for homeless
So if they need to talk, have a meal or just some place to sleep
                                              they can.

Wayne Curry (12)
St Patrick's High School, Keady

Recycling

Pollution is a sin
So use your recycling bin
Your car is made out of tin
Use less paper
Batteries are very toxic
So use your recycling bin.

Hannah Murray (12)
St Patrick's High School, Keady

The Big Green Poetry Machine

Today we must reuse
Or stand to be the accused.
Respect our environment
Don't choose to refuse.
Go green with our team
There is no excuse to throw waste away
The litterbug you should not obey.
Don't abuse the resources of the Earth
Value the Earth for all it's worth.

Ciara McKeown (14)
St Patrick's High School, Lisburn

Going Green

Going green is a fantastic thing
If everyone does it right
It keeps our environment clean
Through day and night!

There are bins in our streets
Though people don't care
The chewing gum and sweets
People pour litter everywhere.

Going green as a team can make our environment a beautiful scene
If you listen to what we say
Simply act today
Everywhere will look as good as new.

Danielle Shannon (13)
St Patrick's High School, Lisburn

The Big Green Poetry Machine

Go green
This is the motto of our team.
Our aim is to look after the Earth
For all that it is worth.
You may have a shock
When the Earth resources go under lock!

The world is being abused
If you choose to refuse
You must feel very confused
Be aware litterbugs
You may be accused!
It's better to share
So why don't you care?

Deborah Anderson (13)
St Patrick's High School, Lisburn

Going Green

The world is going green
Don't delay, start today!
The world is in for a shock
If we don't keep the resources under lock.
Don't abuse the Earth
Then there will be a birth to a new Earth.

Don't take a car or a bus to school
Come and walk today
So let's live our dream
Work together as a team
Come and choose
Don't abuse
Hear our say
Go green today!

Matthew Corken (13)
St Patrick's High School, Lisburn

The Earth Might Burst

Give the Earth the respect it's worth
Or one day it might just burst!
So if you let the world just waste away
You'll wake up and it will be gone some day!
So if you want the world to stay
You'll have to keep your litter at bay.

Ben Portis (12)
St Patrick's High School, Lisburn

Going Green

Going green is the name of our team
We are healthy about the Earth's hygiene!
We share but you must be aware
That we aim to save the Earth
To maintain its worth!
You must now walk away
To try to save the day
You must care and try to share.

Go green with our team
Start to accuse the people who don't reuse
You must care and try to save the Earth.
Don't put your litter on display
You must put it away
And then you can go out to play.

Victoria Dart (13)
St Patrick's High School, Lisburn